T0330572

"Noura Al Obeidli's book is timely and very important. It explores, using a sound method, how patriarchy in the UAE prescribes institutionalized sexism inside the newsroom that disempowers Emirati female journalists. The book makes a fundamental connection between tribalism, media practice, state feminism and patriarchy in the Gulf countries. Al Obeidli's ethnographic study is an excellent contribution to Arab media studies. It is a must-read for anyone researching media practice and gender politics in the Arab region."

Tarik Sabry, *Professor of Media and Cultural Studies,*
University of Westminster

Emirati Women Journalists

This book presents a rare investigation of the media landscape and gender dynamics in Emirati newsrooms, with a socio-cultural focus on the influence of tribal patriarchalism in determining Emirati women's role as newsmakers.

Shedding light on the stories of 40 Emirati and Arab expat journalists, including pioneer Emirati women journalists, the book offers insight into how these journalists construct gender differences and identity and how this influences their everyday attitudes, conversations, routines, and journalistic practices. The empirical study is supplanted with ethnographic explanations of the newsroom norms and journalistic practices from the author, who used participant observation inside two major news centres in Abu Dhabi and Dubai to understand the socio-cultural factors that shape the lives of Emirati and Arab expat journalists, their thoughts and beliefs about the media environment in the Emirates, and their opinions on authoritarian political control, censorship, and outdated media law.

This book will interest students and scholars of journalism and journalistic practice, media policy, international journalism, gender studies, and Middle East studies.

Noura Al Obeidli is a Visiting Assistant Professor of Gender Studies and Media Studies, in the Division of Arts & Humanities within the Interactive Media Program at New York University Abu Dhabi (NYUAD). Her work in the field of feminist media studies began at the University of Westminster, where she defended her doctoral dissertation in April 2020.

Routledge Focus on Journalism Studies

For more information about this series, please visit: https://www.routledge.com/Routledge Focus on Journalism Studies/book-series/RFJS

Emirati Women Journalists

Bargaining with Patriarchy in
Search of Equality

Noura Al Obeidli

LONDON AND NEW YORK

First published 2025
by Routledge
4 Park Square, Milton Park, Abingdon, Oxon OX14 4RN

and by Routledge
605 Third Avenue, New York, NY 10158

Routledge is an imprint of the Taylor & Francis Group, an informa business

British Library Cataloguing-in-Publication Data
A catalogue record for this book is available from the British Library

Library of Congress Cataloging-in-Publication Data
Names: Al Obeidli, Noura, author.
Title: Emirati women journalists : bargaining with patriarchy in search of
equality / Noura Al Obeidli.
Description: Abingdon, Oxon ; New York, NY : Routledge, 2024. | Series:
Routledge focus on journalism studies | Includes bibliographical references
and index.
Identifiers: LCCN 2024015432 (print) | LCCN 2024015433 (ebook) |
ISBN 9781032785417 (hardback) | ISBN 9781032785448 (paperback) |
ISBN 9781003488415 (ebook)
Subjects: LCSH: Women journalists--United Arab Emirates. | Women in
journalism--United Arab Emirates. | Journalism--Social aspects--United
Arab Emirates.
Classification: LCC PN5449.U5 A5 2024 (print) | LCC PN5449.U5 (ebook) |
DDC 305.43/07095357--dc23/eng/20240409
LC record available at https://lccn.loc.gov/2024015432
LC ebook record available at https://lccn.loc.gov/2024015433

ISBN: 978-1-032-78541-7 (hbk)
ISBN: 978-1-032-78544-8 (pbk)
ISBN: 978-1-003-48841-5 (ebk)

DOI: 10.4324/9781003488415

Typeset in Times New Roman
by KnowledgeWorks Global Ltd.

To my dad, whose presence I dearly miss—especially at this milestone. Your love and guidance continue to shape every step I take.

Contents

Acknowledgements

My understanding of journalism reached a new level after I joined the College of Media, Arts and Design at the University of Westminster in London, thanks to the support of my supervisor, Dr. Tarik Sabry. His guidance and advice throughout the development of my doctoral research changed my perspective as an individual and an intellectual. I learned about various Arab and Western gender and media-related studies, which were completely new to me.

Dr. Sabry opened the doors to a whole new world for me through books, theories, and theorists, and the analysis of media, gender, and women from different perspectives, which made me realise the complexity of the social context in which I was born and raised and which shaped me. I am sincerely grateful for his presence in my life, for he was directly responsible for bringing out my hidden self that had been longing to speak out without fear, to think without being petrified of receiving criticism, to make decisions and take action without worrying about social constraints, and to be proud of my heritage and culture—'the culture of giving', as he puts it.

I would also like to thank my family and friends for their motivational support throughout my PhD journey; Dr. Mercedes Bunz and Dr. Roza Tsagarousianou for their significant advice and guidance to improve this doctoral study; Dr. Anthony McNicholas for his assistance with books, studies, and articles related to news sociology; and Dr. David Bulla at Zayed University for his support and feedback in the early stages of this study. Last but not least, I would like to express my gratitude to all the Emirati and Arab expat journalists whose valuable contributions made this doctoral research possible.

Finally, I am deeply grateful to the Humanities Research Fellowship for the Study of the Arab World at NYUAD for their unwavering support throughout my journey in crafting this book. My heartfelt appreciation goes to Dr. Alanood Al Sharekh, Dr. Ildiko Kaposi, Dr. Michael Herb, Dr. Laila Prager, and Dr. May Al Dabbagh for their invaluable guidance and insightful reviews of select chapters, which immensely enriched this work. I extend my sincerest thanks to Dan Geist for his meticulous editing assistance that shaped this manuscript into its final form.

Glossary

asil   Arabic for 'original' or 'noble'; used to describe the elite tribes in the Arab Gulf states, from which the ruling families and other notables are drawn.

ayeb   Arabic for 'shame', connoting—in developmental terms—the cultivation of conformity and fear of others' criticism.

development journalism   A type of journalism which supports government policies and programmes that are designed to build integrated, stable, and economically developed societies.[1]

Emiratisation   A development process that seeks to reduce the reliance on foreign expatriate workers in favour of UAE nationals. It involves not only recruiting UAE nationals to replace expatriates, but also training UAE nationals to acquire skills and competencies desired by employers.

enlightening media   A term often used by journalists interviewed for this study. In this context, it refers to the practise of 'responsible reporting' to highlight news that is relevant to the public interest and the improvement of government services. It also connotes journalists' duty to avoid the invasion of other people's privacy and to instil through responsible reporting the distinctive Emirati social values to preserve national cohesion and the country's political and economic stability.

fitna   An Arabic word that has multiple connotations. From a political perspective, it means trial and war. From a sexual perspective, it means seduction and temptation.

haram   An Arabic word for a forbidden or prohibited act, objects, or conducts.

isnad   A chain of narrators who attest to the historical authenticity of a particular hadith or the prophetic quotes.

Nabatean poetry   Poetry written in Emirati dialect.

Nasserism   Based on the political philosophies of former Egyptian President Gamal Abdel Nasser (1918–1970), 'a system of ideas comprising all or some of the following components: anti-imperialism, pan-Arabism (or nationalism), and Arab socialism'.[2]

Salafism   A hybrid of Wahabism and conservative Islam, Salafism is a revivalist movement formed by Sunni theologians between the 1970s and 1980s, and is still widespread in the Arabian Gulf states.

Trucial States   A group of tribal sheikdoms in the southeastern Arabian Peninsula, such as that of the Al Qawasim tribe, which were party to treaties that established an informal British protectorate from 1820 until 1971.

Wahabism   A revivalist movement formed by Sunni theologians in pursuit of Islamic purity.

wasta   An Arabic term commonly used in the Emirates and Arab Gulf states to refer to an improper scheme or a policy-breaking expedient to gain an advantage.

Notes

1   Allan (2010, p. 149).
2   Podeh et al. (2009, p. 2).

References

Allan, S. (2010). *The Routledge Companion to News and Journalism*. London: Routledge.
Podeh, E. and Winckler, O. (2009). *Rethinking Nasserism*. Tallahassee, Fla.: Orange Grove Texts Plus.

1   Introduction

There's no freedom of the press. We're a tool aimed at promoting the government's initiatives.

—Anonymous Emirati editor, *Abu Dhabi News Centre*

[My mother] used to tell me things like: 'People who join the media have a bad reputation.… I have raised a belly dancer!'

—Rawdha, 35, Emirati journalist, *Zahrat Al Khaleej* magazine

Despite the emergence and pioneering work of three generations of professional journalists in the United Arab Emirates (UAE) since the mid-1960s, views of the media landscape remain cynical. This is due to socio-cultural restraints and political restrictions, amplified by religious and patriarchal perceptions that have been instrumentally embedded in the mindset of Emiratis. Such restraints and perceptions have shaped a distinct Emirati identity, which revolves around tribal homogeneity in the private and collective spheres, and produced a gender gap characterised by specific ideologies and stereotypes and a struggle over women's roles, both public and private.

The complexity of the Emirati media landscape deepened with the introduction of the Publication and Publishing Law by the Ministry of Information and Culture in November 1980, which was formed following the UAE's declaration of independence on 2 December 1971. The articles of the law enumerating penalties for its violation have not been amended since, resulting in the decline of press freedom in the Emirates and extensive self-censorship. This is despite public demands for change to protect Emirati journalists and widespread international criticism of the law.

The distinctive tribal and political environment has made Emirati male and female journalists conscious of their government's main purpose in developing a media industry in the country—to promote the Emirati state's political and economic agenda. This includes sustaining political tribal allegiance and loyalty and improving the country's recognition and reputation on the international scene, especially concerning the empowerment of women.

DOI: 10.4324/9781003488415-1

Censored and criticism-free, all Emirati media platforms have been utilised to champion the government's agenda of empowering Emirati women, which it refers to as nation-building. This agenda is pursued not only primarily through the provision of state-backed education but also by encouraging women's emancipation in the workforce, against all odds, in this patriarchal society. After the first female school was established in 1954, followed by the first female university in 1976,[1] Emirati women began to join professions that were supposedly alien to their natural nurturing roles, which included the newsroom.

However, the government's campaign to empower Emirati women has led to a battle of the sexes inside the workplace, including the newsroom, where various forms of inequality, discrimination, misogyny, sexism, and nepotism are rife. The empowerment campaign has also led to the emergence of state feminism, whose proponents are none other than the neo-traditionalist governing rulers of the seven federal emirates[2] and their wives, who chair most of the government-funded women-focused organisations. This includes the Women's Union, which emphasises Islamic education for Emirati women through lessons, lectures, and conferences focusing on Islam as a faith, well-being, family-related matters and welfare, and general skills improvement. Through an Islamised state feminism that approaches women's educational empowerment with a focus on preserving Emirati society and culture through the promotion of heritage and national cohesion, the government aims to achieve unity, identity-building, and stability, establishing the framework within which women are expected to take up public roles.[3]

Initiating the ethnographic study

Living in a closely guarded patriarchal system has impacted Emirati women's consciousness and self-worth, and many report feeling shame as well as fear of damaging their families' tribal reputation and honour. Patriarchy has also impacted their contribution to public life due to the lack of equal opportunities in various sectors and professional fields, including journalism.

As experienced by female journalists worldwide and documented in previous media studies, entering the newsroom and working in the media industry have proven difficult for Emirati women because of the sexist attitudes and stereotypes held by both Emirati and expat Arab men. As the following chapters reveal, sexism and misogyny inside the newsroom have affected Emirati female journalists' performance, enthusiasm, and initiative to produce hard news stories. Meanwhile, the restrictive policies set by the chief editors (mostly men) at local media corporations have diminished investigative journalism, increased self-censorship, and reduced Emirati female journalists' ability to write about sectors other than childcare, parenting, healthcare, fashion, beauty, and culinary arts, fields viewed as soft and relatively unimportant.

Within this framework, this study was developed after I spent four years studying Emirati women's representation in the media. As an anthropologist, I came to realise that there is scant information on the history of media development and women's contribution to the field of journalism in the Emirates. The only available sources were written in Arabic by non-Emirati historians and published in the early 1980s or mid-1990s, such as Kuwaiti author Layla Salih's *Adab Al Maraa Fi Al Khaleej Al Arabi* (Women's literature in the Arab Gulf; 1983) and Egyptian author Ahmed Nafadi's *Al Sihafa Fi Dowlat Al Emarat Al Arabiya: Tataworat Tarikhiya* (The historical development of journalism in the UAE; 1996). These books treated media development in the Emirates in a descriptive way, listing the newspapers and magazines that were founded in the country since its independence in 1971. A comprehensive discussion of the history of media (both print and broadcast) and the consequences of the publication of the first media law in the Emirates can be found in only two studies: *Al Sihafa Fi Dowal Al Khaleej Al Arabi* (*Journalism in the Arab Gulf States*; 1983), by Iraqi author Azza Ali Ezzat, and *Media Law in the United Arab Emirates* (2014), by American scholar Matt J. Duffy. The present study is thus the first to investigate gender dynamics in Emirati newsrooms, with a focus on the influence of tribal, patriarchal culture in determining Emirati women's role in news media, shedding light on the stories of pioneering Emirati female journalists who struggled socially and culturally to make a mark in this crucial profession. This study is also the first to observe and document the newsroom norms and journalistic practices in the Emirates, which are delimited by an oppressive media law now over 40 years old, authoritarian political control, and censorship.

This study thus answers key research questions that have been used to investigate the socio-cultural challenges that Emirati female journalists endure in a distinctively tribal and patriarchal society, one governed by an authoritarian regime that reinforces state feminism as a form of empowerment for Emirati women and controls all media platforms to protect itself from external threats to its national cohesion and stability. These key research questions evolved around the socio-cultural factors that have challenged Emirati female journalists, the glass ceiling that they have faced in their professional careers, the existing journalistic norms and practices that created a masculine newsroom culture in the Emirates, and the impact of gender inequality on Emirati female journalists' presence in this field.

Two ethnographic methods were applied. The first was participant observation, which took place over four weeks at two government-funded media corporations: Dubai News Centre (Dubai TV), operated by Dubai Media Incorporated, and Abu Dhabi News Centre (Abu Dhabi Channel One), operated by Abu Dhabi Media Company. The second was semi-structured interviews, in which 40 Emirati and Arab expat journalists (25 Emiratis and 15 Arab expats) were interviewed face-to-face. These journalists were categorised based on gender (30 female journalists and 10 male journalists took part) and based on two generational cohorts: journalists from the early generation, who were active between the 1970s and the 1990s and were between the ages of 47 and 65 at the time of their interview; and journalists from the new generation, who were active between the 2000s and the present and were between the ages of 27 and 41 at the time of their interview. Applying the two ethnographic methods took almost four months, during the first half of 2017. These qualitative ethnographic methods were selected with the aim of analysing gender in the newsrooms of the Emirates, how male and female Emirati and Arab expat journalists construct gender differences and identity, and how this influences their everyday attitudes, conversations, routines, and journalistic practices. Through participant observation and semi-structured interviews, this study discusses why journalists practise self-censorship in the newsroom, arguing that the media in the Emirates is engulfed by political oppression and compulsory patriotism.

A synopsis: the historical development of Emirati media

According to one of the Emirates' most prominent journalists, Abdul Ghaffar Hussein, the media in the Trucial States (predecessors to the UAE) was founded five centuries ago by shipmasters who wrote reports for a news digest named *Roznama.*[4] The first shipmaster and navigator to use this method was Shihab Al Din Ahmad Ibn Majid (1430–1500), born in Julfar[5] and fluent in a number of languages, including Urdu, Persian, and Tamil.[6]

Attempts to produce news continued, albeit sporadically, due to the difficult economic conditions during the pre-oil era. During the 1920s and 1930s, wealthy merchants and grocery shop owners such as Ibrahim Mohammed Al Medfaa and Mosabah Obaid Al Dhaheri published two newsletters, *Oman* and *Al Nikhi* (Chickpeas), using modest materials like cuttlefish ink, paper bags, and palm fronds. The newsletters included announcements released by the Sheikh's palace and updates on Arab news copied from regional newspapers—for instance, reports on the political situation in Jerusalem during the British Mandate and the pan-Arab movement led by Haj Mohammed Amin Al Husseini to secure the independence of Palestine.[7]

With the introduction of radio news broadcasts, the 1940s through the early 1960s witnessed growing news production in the Trucial States and the emergence of young male writers influenced by the Arab nationalism movement and demands for independence from British colonialism. Participants in this birth of modern journalism in the region included Humaid Nasser Al Owais and Abdullah Salem Al Omran, who created the *Al Diyar* (Homeland) newspaper in 1961 using stencils instead of conventional typesetting.[8]

The modern press movement in the Emirates has gone through three major stages. The first centred on the relationship with the rulers, who generously allocated budgets to develop the media infrastructure and used it as a tool to support political and economic agendas while avoiding criticism. The second involved an intense media focus on colonisation, typified by criticism of the British protectorate and the political cupidity of the Iranians[9] and Americans in the area after the discovery of oil. The third stage has been dominated by oil, with local media corporations enjoying new profits through the sale of advertising space in dedicated economic supplements, which attracted wealthy merchants and Western companies (mainly car dealers and oil manufacturers) throughout the 1970s and onward.[10] These three stages are discussed at length in Chapter 4.

Meanwhile, educational campaigns dedicated to young girls and women, as well as the launch of state-backed women's associations, provided a sense of empowerment for Emirati women, who began to join the workforce, but in limited numbers. Even after the modernisation of Emirati institutions, Emirati women are, in the main, still relegated to performing traditional duties, sustaining the social values that are rooted in the tribal patriarchal system. Examining the Arab patriarchal apparatus, Palestinian intellectual Hisham Sharabi referred to the new politically modernised system as 'neopatriarchy'. In his 1988 book *Le Néopatriarcat*, he wrote that the processes of modernisation in the Arab world do not render the mechanisms of the patriarchal system obsolete but only dress them up in new garments. Even if the patriarchal system changes its socio-political face, it still sustains a belief in the superiority of men and denies women's rights.[11]

Still, the authoritarian tribal society did not stop state-educated Emirati women from speaking up about their rights through journalism. Early examples include Hessa Al Ossaily, who became the first Emirati radio and television host for Abu Dhabi's stations in 1972; Mouzah Khamis, who became the first Emirati columnist at *Sawt Al Umma* (Voice of the nation) newspaper in 1980; Mouzah Matar, the first Emirati journalist to be recruited by the Sharjah-based *Al Khaleej* newspaper in 1982; and Mariam Youssef, who became the first Emirati media graduate from the College of Communications at Cairo University in 1979. Gradually, the number of Emirati female journalists increased over the 1980s and 1990s, according to the UAE Journalists' Association, reaching 163 by 2014.[12]

Breakdown of chapters

Emirati Women Journalists: Bargaining with Patriarchy in Search of Equality is divided into nine chapters.[13] The first, this introduction, has highlighted the framework of the ethnographic study with an overview of media development in the Emirates, my aims in initiating the study, and the methodologies used to analyse Emirati women's underrepresentation in the media industry and the roles female journalists are constrained to play on behalf of the UAE's nation-building agenda. The introduction has also outlined the socio-cultural perspectives that inform the analysis, which revolve around tribal patriarchalism in the private and collective spheres.

The second chapter, 'The Status of Women: History, Identity, and Gender', contextualises the study and its findings within a theoretical framework to examine the impact of gender, orthodoxy, and strategies of domination on Emirati women's identity and on their socially constructed roles, investigating their participation in the field of media as well as their contribution to creative literature and national development more broadly. In addition, this chapter defines and discusses three powerful notions that underpin this study and are used frequently herein to illuminate the social composition and socio-political systems of, as well as gender discourse within, Arab Gulf societies in general and Emirati society in particular: tribalism, patriarchy, and gender.

The third chapter, 'Ethnography in the Newsroom', explains the study's qualitative methodology, conceived to investigate specific issues about media in the Emirates that remain significantly underexamined. Using two interrelated qualitative approaches, I gathered a significant amount of evidence to provide an in-depth picture of the region's complex gender dynamics and their association with the social constructs of Emirati tribal culture. I have also analysed the influence of these social constructs on the media landscape in the Emirates, which is seen as necessarily patriotic and loyal to the state. The observations and interviews reveal how gender and authoritarianism dictate journalistic practices and routines in the newsroom, where *a priori* censorship is commonplace and institutional barriers limit Emirati women journalists' progress in the field. The chapter describes the challenges encountered in the evidence gathering, including how a number of journalists declined participation in the semi-structured interviews for fear of the consequences of voicing their concerns about self-censorship, the UAE's oppressive media law, and enduring sexism in the newsroom.

Before the book turns to the findings of the observations and the semi-structured interviews, the fourth chapter, 'The Media Landscape and State Control', surveys the history of government control over the media and how news production and newsroom practices at Abu Dhabi and Dubai media outlets arose and developed. It examines the code of ethics and journalism practices in the Emirates and analyses the media industry as an employer with regard to the practice of 'shadowing', in which expat journalists, Arabs included, teach journalism to Emirati journalists from their own perspective, bringing to the fore the differences in their prior journalistic experiences. These could involve working under a dictatorship that forced them to practise self-censorship in the newsroom.

Historically, the media environment in the Emirates has been seen as oppressive and unrepresentative due to the government's surveillance and control over publications, leading the majority of journalists, men and women, locals and expats alike, to feel intimidated and practise self-censorship. The state exercises political and financial power, in particular, by directing top media corporations' officials, in both the Arabic and English-language press, in how to produce news and what type of content to publish—a state of affairs discussed in this chapter using evidence, including the penalties set forth in the 1980 media law.

The fifth chapter, 'The Ultimate Question: Who's in Charge?', analyses the first part of the study's findings concerning gendered newsroom practices and contrasts Emirati women's experience in journalism with that of their female counterparts elsewhere. It illuminates the variety of ways in which newsroom practices are gendered and investigates the socio-cultural restrictions and institutionalised gender clustering and sexism inside the newsroom that disempower Emirati female journalists and put them at a disadvantage in relation to their male colleagues.

The sixth chapter, 'Journalists at Odds over Censorship, Language, and PR Influence', turns to the second part of the study's findings, concerning non-gendered newsroom practices. The observations and semi-structured interviews with 40 Emirati and Arab expat journalists explain how freedom of expression is overwhelmed by self-censorship because of socio-political influences that force them to act cautiously and how they are affected by the dominance of PR firms in the country, resulting in the creation of news content that is invariably loyal, patriotic, repetitive, and promotional.

The seventh chapter, 'Tribalism and the Female Journalists' Voice: A Dilemma Overlooked', analyses the third part of the findings, which focus on how gender as an identity marker intersects with others, such as tribe, family, and class in the Emirates. It also considers the impact of tribal patriarchalism as a socio-political system imposed on Emirati journalists. Data are presented that reflect respondents' experiences in terms of their bargaining with patriarchy.

The eighth chapter, 'State Feminism: Empowerment, Gender Balance, and Nation-Branding', analyses the fourth and final part of the findings. It explains the historical progression of Emirati women's societal role prior to the nation-building scheme and addresses the anomalies that have arisen with the state's approach to empowering Emirati women whilst holding on to tradition in the face of rapid social change. Emirati women are rendered carriers of the so-called traditions that those in power select and reinvent to suit their own purposes. While state-backed empowerment campaigns for education and the employment of Emirati women started soon after the country's federal union on 2 December 1971, they have not been fully absorbed by the resilient tribal patriarchal society.

The book's conclusion examines the findings against the backdrop of the formation of the tribal patriarchal system in the Emirates and its particular ramifications for Emirati female journalists. It looks at the influence of this system in shaping a distinct Emirati mindset and gender roles within a unique socio-cultural framework, and thus in creating a distinctive media culture with ethical principles and norms that are very different from those of the media culture in the West.

Notes

1 Ghazal (2014).
2 The seven federal emirates are (in descending order of political power): Abu Dhabi, Dubai, Sharjah, Ajman, Umm Al Qaiwain, Ras Al Khaimah, and Fujairah.
3 Krause (2009).
4 Persian for 'calendar'.
5 Today the northern emirate of Ras Al Khaimah.
6 Salamah (2005, pp. 38–47).
7 Obaid (2000).
8 Nafadi (1996).
9 The Iranians clung to the historical fact that the Gulf was identified as Persian, not Arabian, and the name dispute was evident in newspaper coverage of the era (Ezzat, 1983, p. 100).
10 Ezzat (1983).
11 Al Oraimi (2011, p. 85).
12 Al Bakour (2014).
13 The book's subtitle was inspired by Deniz Kandiyoti's articles 'Bargaining with Patriarchy: Gender and Society' (1988) and 'Gender, Power and Contestation: Rethinking Bargaining with Patriarchy' (1998).

References

Al Bakour, B. (2014). 'Emirati Female Journalists Moving Forward'. *Al Hayat*. Translated by the author. Available at: http://www.alhayat.com/Articles/2058535/ [Accessed 17 September 2017].

Al Oraimi, S. (2011). 'The Concept of Gender in Emirati Culture: An Analytical Study of the Role of the State in Redefining Gender and Social Roles', *Museum International*, 63(3–4), pp. 78–92.

Ezzat, A. (1983). *Journalism in the Arab Gulf States*. Translated by the author. Baghdad: Gulf States Information Documentation Centre.

Ghazal, R. (2014). 'History Project: Girls' Schools in a Class of Their Own'. *The National*. 1 December. Available at: https://www.thenational.ae/uae/heritage/history-project-girls-schools-in-a-class-of-their-own-1.271865 [Accessed 12 April 2019].

Krause, W. (2009). 'Gender and Participation in the Arab Gulf'. *London School of Economics Research Online*. September. Available at: http://eprints.lse.ac.uk/55255/1/Krause_2009.pdf [Accessed 8 May 2019].

Nafadi, A. (1996). *Journalism in the UAE: Origins, Technical and Historical Evolution*. Translated by the author. Abu Dhabi: UAE's Cultural Foundation Publications.

Obaid, A. (2000). 'Journalism in the UAE from Beginnings to Global Horizons'. *Al Bayan*, 18 April. Translated by the author. Available at: http://www.albayan.ae/one-world/2000-04-18-1.1083118 [Accessed 3 June 2013].

Salamah, S. (2005). 'Journalism in the UAE Qualitative Leap in Record Time'. *Al Turath*. 83rd edn. Translated by the author. Abu Dhabi: Sultan bin Zayed Cultural Centre Publications, October, pp. 38–47.

2   The Status of Women

History, Identity, and Gender

Understanding the complexities of the media environment and journalistic practice in the Emirates requires an anthropological engagement with the country's
political identity and ambitions, its social values, culture, and heritage—all
deeply influenced by Islam. Every aspect of Emirati life reflects the dominance of
this orthodoxy, including political practice, law-making, inheritance, ownership,
decision-making, and above all, hierarchy, resulting in an authoritative, tribal, and
patriarchal society that is often in conflict with modernity.

As a consequence, news-making in the Emirates is inextricably linked with a
particular religious and political identity that revolves around patriotism, nationalism, and loyalty to authority. All media platforms, including social and other
digital media, are integrated to function not only as a univocal source of news information but also as a univocal source of guidance—instilling national identity
discourses, emphasising the importance of preserving the UAE's unique culture
and traditions, and maintaining its social cohesion to sustain the national identity,
political solidarity, peace, and security.

This chapter contextualises the study and its findings within a theoretical
framework, with the aim of examining the impact of news-making, religion, and
political identity on women's comprehension of their identity and socially constructed roles and to investigate their participation in the field of media as well as
their contribution to creative literature and national development in general. To
this end, the chapter addresses three key themes: tribalism and family in the Gulf;
women, journalism, and newsroom practices; and women and nation-building. It
is important first to define and discuss three powerful notions that underpin this
study and will be used frequently to explicate the social composition and socio-
political systems of, as well as gender discourse within, the Arab Gulf societies as
a whole and Emirati society in particular: tribalism, patriarchy, and gender.

Defining tribalism, patriarchy, and gender

The basic social composition of the Arab Gulf states comprises two categories of
tribes that are distinguished by distinctive genealogies, political allies, and economic power, and a third, nontribal category. The first category is the *asil* tribes,
or the ascriptive elite, who claim recognised descent from noble or pure tribes,

DOI: 10.4324/9781003488415-2

however distant in the past. The ruling families and urban notables, as well as Bedouins of pure descent, belong to this category, associated with wealth, education, and social prestige.[1] The second category is the non-*asil* tribes, who can trace their descent to a subordinate tribe and have close ties and relations with the ruling families that are often sealed by politically arranged marriages to strengthen tribal loyalty. They are known for their considerable amount of wealth due to their status in the non-oil era as merchants and hold prominent positions in today's monarchical states, such as the Al Attiya family in Qatar.[2] The third and final category is the nontribal population—known as *khadiri*[3] in the Arab Gulf region—who cannot trace their descent to a tribe, such as Shia Muslims, those of African descent, Sunnis of forgotten origins, and immigrants.

The discovery of oil, followed by an economic boom and progress in education and healthcare, altered the social composition of Arab Gulf societies and introduced stratification based on social class. The *asil* tribes dominate the top of the social pyramid, while the nontribal population, much fewer in number, dominates the bottom of the social pyramid and comprises groups such as the Shia Muslims and the *bidoon* (those without citizenship or stateless).[4] They are able to receive only temporary passports and are excluded from employment in the public sector.[5] The latter also includes the Baluch people, whose ancestors migrated from the Baluchistan region of Pakistan.[6]

The middle class at the centre of the social pyramid comprises the non-*asil* or subordinate tribes, who are privileged by enjoying free education funded by the state. This particular privilege has resulted in the formation of a large group of intellectuals and advocates for reform in the Arab Gulf states. They benefit from privileged employment at prominent state establishments and enjoy high pay and financial security. Such privileges have earned the middle-class social recognition and integration with the upper class, including the monarchy, which they do not oppose as a political system or threaten to overthrow. This allegiance owes in part to Arab Gulf monarchs' having taken steps to reform politics after independence, most importantly, holding fair elections and appointing women as state ministers. A monarchical path to democracy is characterised by such steps.[7]

This idiosyncratic stratification based on tribal class has shaped the state-society relationship in the Arab Gulf states, impacting the role of the media and limiting public opinion. The authoritarian leaders of the Arab Gulf states control the state-society relationship and obtain loyalty amongst supporters from the *asil* and non-*asil* tribes by allocating economic resources in the form of private or public goods, lowering tax rates, and distributing wealth in the form of income or high pay across society.[8] This type of control, also practised in other authoritarian regimes, like China and Singapore, minimises public demands and facilitates public support for the political system. Male and female journalists alike have been instrumental in encouraging support for this system, both to safeguard their own economic interests and to avoid 'the coercive arm of the state'[9] being brought into action, as described by political scientist Shirin Rai. As a result, male and female journalists are forced to practice self-censorship so as not to publish news that crosses 'fuzzy red lines'[10] in fear of imprisonment or deportation.

Nevertheless, the authoritarian leaders' control over the production and content of news in the Arab Gulf states has opened the way towards advancing the status of women through their empowerment. Projecting women's empowerment in every vital sector, including journalism, has become part of the Arab Gulf states' nation-branding schemes to position themselves favourably on the international scene. Nation-branding reframes national identity, culture, and governance to enhance the competitive advantage of nations in a global market environment. Through this form of state propaganda, 'government narratives are addressed to the international community for the sake of polishing and improving their reputation'[11] as well as to position themselves favourably, rather than—for instance—reflecting real efforts to support the position of women, a matter investigated in detail in the following chapters.

The second notion that needs to be defined and discussed is patriarchy. In Walby's *Theorizing Patriarchy*, she cites Max Weber's definition of patriarchy as 'a system of government in which men ruled societies through their position as heads of households' and adds her own definition, according to which patriarchy is 'a system of social structures and practises in which men dominate, oppress and exploit women'.[12]

In investigating the system of patriarchy, Walby has categorised it into six so-cial structures. The first is the patriarchal mode of production, in which 'women's household labour is expropriated by their husbands' and in which housewives are considered 'the producing class, while husbands are the expropriating class'.[13] The second is 'patriarchal relations in paid work', in which women are excluded from 'the better forms of work' and given the 'worse jobs' which are seen as requiring less skill.[14] Patriarchal relations in the state is third, with the state having 'a sys-tematic bias towards patriarchal interests in its policies and actions',[15] making it both capitalist and racist. The fourth structure is male violence, in which forms of male aggression such as 'rape, wife beating, and sexual harassment' are 'systemati-cally ignored and legitimated by the state's refusal to intervene except in excep-tional instances'.[16] Patriarchal relations in sexuality is fifth, in which the patriarchal system has determined that heterosexuality is and should be the norm; and sixth is patriarchal relations in cultural institutions, which 'create the representation of women within a patriarchal gaze' in diverse fields such as religion, education, and the media.[17]

The social construction of women's roles and its relation to patriarchy high-lights the role of state-backed empowerment campaigns in moulding the social status of women in the Arab Gulf states generally, and in the Emirates specifically, while advancing it through the advocacy of women's rights in education, legisla-tion, and employment. Yet these social advances have been applied top-down and directly regulated by the state, making social change for Emirati women, in par-ticular, challenging due to the direct involvement of the patriarchs in their lives, making it impossible for them to attain personal and professional autonomy.

The third and final notion that needs to be defined and discussed is gender. 'Gender is a concept that refers to a system of roles and relationships between women and men which are determined not by biology, but by the social, political and economic context'.[18] It is also, as Naila Kabeer describes, a 'process by which individuals who are born into biological categories of male or female become the social categories of men and women through the acquisition of locally defined attributes of masculinity and femininity'.[19] Theorist Judith Butler explains that gender is fabricated, constructed, and sustained as a way of life, defining it as 'an identity tenuously constituted in time, instituted in an exterior space through a *stylized repetition of acts…*. The effort of gender is produced through the stylization of the body and, hence, must be understood as the mundane way in which bodily gestures, movements, and styles of various kinds constitute the illusion of an abiding gendered life'.[20]

Investigations of gender identity as a construct have led many sociologists, including Chris Jenks, to associate the progress of the human mind with the evolution of culture in human civilisation. In 2003, Jenks argued that culture has taken three forms throughout history. The first is the 'ideal, in which culture is a state or process of human perfection in terms of certain absolute or universal values'.[21] The second is 'documentary, in which culture is the body of intellectual and imaginative work and in which human thought and experience are variously recorded'.[22] The third is 'social, in which culture is a description of a particular way of life, which expresses certain meanings and values not only in art and learning but also in institutions and ordinary behaviour'.[23] The social construction of culture has led to the formation of distinct, socially constructed gender identities in which roles and responsibilities, contributions, and expectations were defined based on stratification, and in which 'male-supremacist cultural expressions',[24] as explained by Karl Marx, were invented and integrated into spiritual myths, rituals, arts, and literature. As such, gender identities have been universally influenced by cultural notions that are based on power relations and strategies of domination that cast women as subordinate by biology and nature, with less valued physical and psychological attributes than men.

There is evidence, however, of egalitarianism practised before this cultural evolution by Neolithic societies, such as in Çatalhöyük in southern Anatolia (7000 BCE). In her anthropological study of Neolithic societies, Elise Boulding explained that

> each sex developed appropriate skills and knowledge essential for group survival. Woman knew how to transform the raw materials and dead animals into nurturing products. Her skills must have been as manifold as those of man and certainly as essential. Woman, in pre-civilized society, must have been man's equal and may well have felt herself to be his superior.[25]

From ancient times to the Middle Ages, through the rise of feminist movements in the 18th century, philosophers, existentialists, and psychoanalysts have produced different hypotheses to explain the emergence of power relations, in particular, ones based on psychological perspectives of male supremacy and dominance. Sigmund Freud argued that male aggression drove men to build civilization, and feminist theorist Simone de Beauvoir emphasised biology as the basis of male supremacy. As Gerda Lerner has observed, a group of theorists, including Susan Brownmiller, Elizabeth Fisher, and Mary O'Brien, argued that 'the domestication of animals taught men their role in procreation and that the practice of the forced mating of animals led men to the idea of rape'[26] as a means to demonstrate their superiority and dominance. And thus, biological and psychological male aggression, in parallel with the development of patriarchy and militarism as a result of intertribal feuds, increased men's tendency to exercise authority over women. Referencing sociologist Elise Boulding's work, Lerner writes that women nonetheless played crucial roles in the socio-political affairs of patriarchal tribal societies, including negotiations over the trading of women themselves. Women, she suggests, were able to 'develop cultural flexibility and sophistication by their intertribal linkage role' and could 'straddle two cultures and learn the ways of both'.[27]

Numerous psychoanalytical studies have described the formation of gendered personalities based on the concepts of superiority and inferiority—for example, man as a 'noble sex' and woman as 'incidental being' or 'imperfect man', as characterized by St. Thomas.[28] Other studies have examined the way that historically certain social roles have been envisaged for women, like motherhood and the functions of the obedient daughter and wife. When it comes to motherhood, sociologist Nancy Chodorow has claimed that, from an early age, boys' and girls' relationships with their parents differs in significant ways:

> To find their identity, boys develop themselves as other-than-the-mother; they identify with the father and turn away from emotional expression toward action in the world. Growing girls come to define and experience themselves as continuous with others; their experience of self contains more flexible or permeable ego boundaries.[29]

By doing so, as Chodorow claimed, the male and female child come to define selfhood differently and form an ego that establishes a hierarchy of the sexes. Sociologist Pierre Bourdieu made a similar observation. In *La domination masculine*, he argued that boys are encouraged to 'break with the maternal world, from which girls are exempted—which enables them to live in a kind of continuity with their mothers'.[30]

As for girls, personal development is more problematic since socio-cultural—and religious—subordination is not only imposed on their gender but also on their bodies, which are viewed and treated by men as sacred, *fitna*,[31] and *haram*.[32] This weighs them down psychologically, from the age they enter puberty through adolescence to womanhood, limiting their experiences and opportunities in life. They are nurtured with a belief in male superiority and prestige and that their bodies will be subjected to 'male conquest',[33] as argued by Ania Loomba.

Universally, women have carried the dual burdens of the feminine body and the feminine gender. Those who resisted the patriarchal system and male dominance, like Eastern and Western feminists and existentialists, called for consciousness-raising against discrimination and pursued equal access to power, rights, and influence. But most of these individuals suffered, such as Doria Shafiq, a pioneering

Egyptian journalist, political activist, and feminist thinker who was labelled by her opponents as the 'Marron Glacé Boss'.[34] Shafiq was put under house arrest by Gamal Abdul Nasser's regime for 18 years as a consequence of an 11-day food strike that she organised in 1957. The strike was against what she described to the press as Nasser's dictatorship, his incompetence in running the nation's political and economic affairs, and his bid to undermine women's rights, and she demanded his resignation. Isolated, criticised, unemployed, and denied her right to free speech, Shafiq threw herself from the sixth-floor balcony of her flat, committing suicide in September 1975.[35] Her legacy remains provocative, to the extent that her name was removed from school textbooks during the presidency of Mohammad Morsi, who was backed by the Muslim Brotherhood.[36]

Early history of tribalism and women

To comprehend this ethnographic study, it is necessary to unpack how the historical tribal Muslim community spanning the Gulf, the Arabian Peninsula, and particularly the Emirates evolved into 20th-century patriarchal nations empowered by unprecedented levels of wealth, fuelled by the discovery of oil. Before and after the emergence of Islam, tribes,[37] or *qabael*, in the Emirates, as well as elsewhere in the Arabian Peninsula (excluding the MENA region due to major differences in their formation and cultural characteristics), were divided into three groups. These were coastal tribes, mountain tribes, and desert tribes, each with distinctive genealogies, traditions, rituals, and philosophies that endowed their members with pride and dignity or shame and dishonour. An example of proud ancestry is the Bani Murrah tribe, which traces its lineage back to a famous figure named Murrah, who lived before the Prophet.[38] An example of a less privileged ancestry would be the mountain tribe of Bani Riyam, who lost their reputation and position as one of the most important tribes in the area after planning a failed coup against the former Sultan of Oman in 1959.[39]

Moreover, the people of the Arabian Peninsula and Trucial States (the Emirates today) were isolated from the rest of the region and had little communication from farther afield. The political and economic atmosphere was permeated with tribal feuds and disputes over leadership and land. The few foreign visitors included missionaries who aimed to evangelise the Peninsula,[40] such as The Wheel from the United States, whose volunteers, led by Reverend Samuel Zwemer of New Jersey, had travelled the desert in search of nomads since 1889.[41] There were also adventurous Western explorers who were drawn by the mystique of the Arabian Desert and the Bedouins' traditions and hospitality. These famously included Thomas Edward Lawrence, known as Lawrence of Arabia, and Sir Wilfred Patrick Thesiger, known as Mubarak bin London. Meanwhile, the British colonial presence along the Peninsula's coastline was minimal, aimed at maintaining control of the naval route from the Persian Sea passage to the Strait of Hormuz and the open ocean that led to other British colonies. The Peninsula was an arid zone, mapped as the Empty Quarter. Its inhabitants were Bedu—Bedouins, as labelled by the colonisers—who were stereotypically represented, as described by Emirati author Mohammed Al Murr in *Life Is Given and Life Is Taken Away* (1998), as 'sinister harbingers of violence and banditry'.[42]

Yet the people of the Arabian Peninsula and the Trucial States were distinguished for their tribal loyalty, which was linked by patrilineal ties to religion, tradition, and heritage. Women of the Arabian Peninsula and the Trucial States were restricted to preserving and maintaining one particular social norm within the tribe, honour (*sharaf* in Arabic), which had to be reflected in their manners as family members, married women, mothers, and supporters of their husbands in all the complementary work that they took part in outside the home to survive, such as selling clothes, food, and fish. In his memoir *The Arab of the Desert* (1949), British Lieutenant Colonel Harold Richard Patrick Dickson observed of the tribal custom of honour: 'True it is that you can make a Badawin man or woman do pretty well anything in this world except sacrifice his or her honor, by the offer of money'.[43]

The influence of tribal honour and other norms for countless generations, even before the dawn of Islam in the Peninsula and the reforms that the Prophet Muhammad introduced, made women submissive. Downing and Roush (1985) referred to women's social behaviour as 'passive acceptance',[44] in which women come to believe that they are inferior, secondary to men, and accustom themselves to traditional duties. The Emirati tribes, though subjected to various external political and economic pressures during the long history of the British protectorate (from 1820 until 1971), were able to preserve tribal honour and cohesion, a central pillar in the protection of genealogical identity. Internal political, social, and economic complications were resolved amongst the senior members of a tribe as if it were a family affair. Women, too, were included in the discussions and decision-making processes, albeit behind the scenes, especially in terms of arranging intermarriages for tribal political allegiances, which clearly indicates that tribalism in the Emirates was both patriarchal and matriarchal.

Next to tribal cohesion, orthodoxy comes second as a pillar in the moral affinities of all tribes in the Emirates, making significant departures from ancient traditional practices and customs difficult for the new generation, especially women. Many of the repressive laws against women were introduced and reproduced by tribal customs and practices that predate Islam. An example of religious equality was even observed during the Prophet's time, when men and women gathered in mosques for prayer and attended political assemblies for consultation (known legally as *shura*) without segregation.[45]

Segregation and veiling were widespread customs that tribal societies in the Arabian Peninsula imposed on women, even before the dawn of Islam. Indeed, Muhammad advised women to dress modestly only because men treated them as sexual commodities and concubines during the pre-Islamic period. This is in conflict with how some Eastern and Western Orientalists and theologians have interpreted this particular phenomenon, such as the Earl of Cromer, who censured the low status of Muslim women in order to criticise Islam as a religion in general.[46] Criticism of the religion and its association with the low status of women, in particular, continued throughout the 20th century. For instance, Iranian writer Sadegh Hedayat, who sought salvation in embracing the Zoroastrian faith, wrote: 'Every aspect of life and thought, including women's condition, changed after Islam. En-slaved by men, women were confined to the home'.[47]

Advocates of Islam have defended the scripture and prophetical tradition that were originally initiated to foster tolerance. For example, in his 13th-century book *Rawdat Al Muhibbin* (Garden of lovers), Imam Ibn Qayyim explained with Quranic evidence that men were created weak by God, unable to resist women's appeals and charms.[48] Gender segregation and veiling in tribal societies, which is still in practice today, albeit minimally in modern Arab and Muslim societies, was in fact developed as a fashionable practice in ancient Persia and was soon adopted as a sign of esteem and reputation by the Muslims, Christians, and Jews of the upper class who settled in the Arab East and the Arabian Peninsula.[49] Such practices were further anchored by the widespread presence of extreme Islamic theologies such as Salafism,[50] followed by Wahabism[51] in the 18th century, and were embraced by the tribal societies, generation after generation, in the Arabian Peninsula and the Emirates, remaining intact in the face of modernity through the mid-20th century.[52]

Lebanese scholar Layal Ftouni explains that, influenced by the thoughts of the Wahhabi scholars in the Arab Gulf states, the patriarchal male elite deployed the science of *isnad*[53] to interpret the Prophet's Hadith and the Quranic *suras* in a manner that served their own political and sexual interests.[54] She observes that the notion that hijab and strict gender segregation are essential to Islam 'is a patriarchal fabrication that was later maintained during the colonial period by Arab nationalists, and is maintained today by some Islamist groups as a way to secure their dominion in the face of change'.[55] However, the newfound oil wealth dramatically changed the conditions and lifestyle of Emirati tribal society, which reaped benefits from the government such as free education, inexpensive housing and healthcare services, and employment opportunities. This change has resulted in an exodus by many tribes from the interior desert and oases to settlements, replacing tribal cohesion as a social unit with a Western model of the modern family. Free education and employment opportunities, along with the government's social campaigns to empower women and establish a gender-equal society (which started in the early 1970s), have extended the tribal society's comprehension of the outside world and their acceptance, albeit gradual, of women's breaking from traditional roles, joining the workforce as equal partners, and speaking up in all matters that affect the country's growth and progress.[56]

Nonetheless, Emirati women cannot depend solely on state-backed campaigns for their empowerment, especially with the increase in Emirati women's participation in politics and the launch of the Gender Balance Council. Based on the ethnographic findings of this study, discussed at length in the following chapters, these campaigns are deficient for a number of reasons. First, most opportunities for emancipation in the Emirates are reserved for upper-class women with strong familial, particularly male, networks that are close to the royal court. Second, the state campaigns are being pressured by the international community's standards of gender equality, which are ignorant of complex, predominantly domestic, labour, and legal issues. Third, there is inadequate education in gender studies, which is excluded from the school curriculum, impeding efforts to close the gender gap in the Emirates. Fourth is the persistent refusal to reinterpret the *tafasir* literature of Islamic scholars and to re-examine religious scripture in order to adopt new policies on women's rights. The fifth, final reason, is Emirati women's resistance to learning and raising awareness about their own rights, which has created a divide and made many Emirati women even more fervent than Emirati men in upholding patriarchal values and prejudices.

Under these circumstances, orthodoxy and the tribal patriarchal culture are still influencing the political, economic, and social spheres in the Arab Gulf states, in general, and the Emirates, in particular. They maintain a tight grip on Emirati people's minds and control the development of ethical and professional practices in crucial fields such as journalism, delaying the Emirati people's progress towards freedom of expression and choice and thwarting the full empowerment of Emirati women.

The rise of women in media: Torn between tradition and opportunity

In the oil-rich Arab Gulf states, the achievement of absolute gender equality is still considered a political aspiration only by its opponents, for it is overshadowed in patriarchal societies by enshrined gender-defined roles, expectations, and socio-cultural norms, which are often given religious legitimacy. The culture of tribalism in these states, including the Emirates, has produced power relations and strategies for domination that subordinate women. These impact women's ability to act as decision-makers in terms of being solely responsible for their own choices in life. The results create ongoing conflict over their role in various fields, particularly in journalism, where societal norms are deeply embedded within mainstream cultural institutions that uphold patriarchy and privilege men's experiences. As a consequence, women's expertise, interests, and issues are limited to the private sphere.[57]

The emergence of women's liberation movements in some Arab Gulf states, like Kuwait, has allowed women journalists to resist tribal patriarchal oppression by voicing their concerns openly over women's political participation and civil rights. However, some have met with grave consequences owing to their deviations from socio-cultural norms. For instance, Hidaya Al Salem (1936–2001), one of Kuwait's pioneer women journalists and a feminist and chief editor of *Al Majalis*[58] magazine, was shot by a policeman while she was on her way to a conference organised by the Women's Association of Kuwait. The murder was motivated by tribal honour, as a column she wrote was perceived to have insulted the women of the Al Awazem tribe.[59] The lack of free will and free speech, as exemplified by the case of Al Salem, has disempowered women journalists and led to the retrenchment of journalism practices. This was described by the Arab Human Development Report, published in 2002 with the support of the United Nations, which found that women's voices, in particular, were stifled.

Another form of oppression to which Arab Gulf women are subjected has been brought to light, pertaining not to economic or political life, but rather to their psychological status. According to professor Sandra Bartky (referencing Patricia Illingworth), 'psychological oppression can be regarded as the "internalization of intimations of inferiority"'.[60] Bartky elaborates: 'Psychological oppression is institutionalized and systematic; it serves to make the work of domination easier by breaking the spirit of the dominated'.[61] Attempts to launch feminist movements and nongovernmental organisations by pioneer female journalists and intellectuals to secure women's political and legal rights in the Arab Gulf states did not change the socially constructed patriarchal ideologies that interpreted the male-female relation as the oppressor versus the oppressed, the superior versus the inferior. In Kuwait, for instance, journalist and activist Nouria Al Saddani established the Arab Women's Development Society (AWDS) in 1963. Its aims were to challenge tribal and social structures, demand women's rights in education and political practice, and call for changes in women's status within Kuwaiti family law. Al Saddani's activism raised awareness amongst upper- and middle-class Kuwaiti women, and the impact of her work promoting gender equality and radical feminism spread fear amongst opponents, especially amongst the extreme Sunni fundamentalists, or Salafis. As a result, AWDS was closed down by the government, and Al Saddani was forced into exile in 1975.[62]

The emergence of capitalism and technologically advanced societies, in which Arab Gulf women were granted education and employment opportunities to varying degrees by the state, have only increased their exposure to sexism, particularly in the form of verbal harassment, which will be covered in the findings chapters. They also experienced discrimination and misogyny that negatively influenced their performance, creativity, and aspirations by forcing them into customary submission to patriarchal norms. This is evident in one of the most sought-after professions, media (print and broadcast), where women's sexuality is exploited while at the same time, their creative outputs and their voices are continually silenced by men, who maintain a dominant hold on the field worldwide. Many stories on this subject have emerged from the Middle East, where still dominant patriarchal ideologies influence the sociology of news production and the portrayal of Arab women in the news. For instance, when Lebanon launched the LBC and Future satellite television channels in 1996, executives hired female anchors 'in low-cut attire in a bid to woo Arab Gulf audiences, who were unaccustomed to seeing women on their own television screens'.[63] Future TV anchor Najat Sharrafeddine recalled 'a Lebanese director telling female presenters that viewers wanted to see them, not listen to them. Gibran Tueni once told one of his reporters on Al Nahar that TV works according to the star system, empowering women through their beauty'.[64]

In the developed, fundamentalist, and tribal Arab Gulf nations, women's representation in the media is also inadequate, while their creative output is restricted and mostly invisible due to the prevailing patriarchal culture and social norms that are influenced by the dominant religion, Islam. As I argue in the following chapters, Emirati women's inadequate representation in the media is the product of more than just factors specific to their patriarchal society. Four more universal key factors are basic gender stereotyping, limited opportunities to hold leading positions within media corporations, horizontal segregation, and gender clustering inside the newsroom.

The female journalism workforce in Western countries is not immune to these factors, as author Suzanne Franks debated in her book *Women and Journalism*. In the United Kingdom, for instance, female journalists who succeed in reporting political news are often mistreated and can be viewed by their male peers as either newshounds or soft-featured bunnies.[65] A pervasive bullying culture has affected the mental health and performance of female journalists, including Emirati ones, as the findings chapters will discuss. These women, especially those who want to cover politics or economics, feel pressured to submit to the prevailing masculine newsroom practices, as documented in a report published by the International Women's Media Foundation in 2000.[66]

Another dominant factor is the practice of censorship in the Arab Gulf states' media corporations, including international media agencies. In these organisations, male and female journalists adhere to the practice of self-censorship. Every media platform is used by the Arab Gulf states' authoritarian regimes as a propaganda tool to control the flow of news and guide public opinion to maintain political stability within their societies. As noted in the 2021 World Press Freedom Index, all of the six monarchical states' rankings in the World Press Freedom Index, as compiled by Reporters without Borders, have dropped recently, with Kuwait in 105th position. The Emirates, Qatar, and Oman were ranked below dozens of African dictatorships in the 131st, 128th, and 133rd positions, respectively. Saudi Arabia and Bahrain were ranked amongst the very worst countries in the world in 170th and 168th positions, respectively.[67]

The censorship strategies used in the Arab Gulf states include both physical and digital surveillance, internet filtering, and censorship departments' monitoring of local media corporations as well as international media agencies. Fear and fierce criticism of these strategies have been expressed not only by international media observers but by locals and resident expats as well. A poll commissioned by the BBC's Doha Debates in 2011, however, revealed that more than half of the Gulf respondents were 'too afraid to speak out against their rulers'. In the same poll, meanwhile, citizens of North African Arab Spring states expressed optimism about their freedoms.[68] Unlike other Arab Gulf states such as Bahrain and Saudi Arabia that use violence and brutality to stifle the voices of their people, the UAE has implemented vigilant schemes to control the media because, as Davidson pointed out, its non-oil economic sectors such as tourism rely increasingly on maintaining a sound international reputation.[69]

After eliminating an article authorising the imprisonment of journalists in 2009 from the media law first instituted in 1980, the Emirates introduced a new regulation to pressure journalists and media corporations by ordering massive fines if they cross the red lines by, for example, 'disparaging senior government officials or the royal family' or 'misleading the public and harming the economy'.[70] Reporting on the new regulation, Human Rights Watch (2009) stated that it restricted 'free expression and would unduly interfere with the media's ability to report on sensitive subject', adding that the law 'includes provisions that would grant the government virtually complete control in deciding who is allowed to work as a journalist and which media organizations are allowed to operate in the country'.[71]

Symbolising women through the state media

Arab media studies have produced a compendium of research on media, culture, and society in the Arab region and the wider Middle East, yet little research has been conducted on the nature of news cultures in the Arab Gulf, an area often overlooked by scholars, with little Western press coverage on its restricted media law, journalism, and censorship practices. In the Arab Gulf, the practice of journalism differs from that of the Middle East and the West, where speech and the press are considerably freer. The dominance of authoritarianism in the Arab Gulf has instilled an awareness of nationalism and patriotic values in journalists. These values explicitly define the news culture in the Emirates, influencing journalistic practices, manipulating the representation of women as a symbol of an idealised femininity, and Islamising feminism through pro-state propaganda and projects, an underexamined phenomenon investigated in this study. Theorists have produced different definitions of nationalism.

Nationalism is a crucial propaganda tool, often used as a governmental mechanism in Emirati mass media outlets and technologies to maintain the state's political power, unify public opinion with that of the authoritarian state, and protect society from external threats and crises. This was the case in the Emirati press during the time of the Iranian revolution in 1979, driven by fear of Shiite power expansion; during Saddam Hussein's invasion of Kuwait in 1990; and, more recently, during the aftermath of the 2010 Arab Spring, which saw the deepening of the divide between Sunnis and Shiites in Saudi Arabia and Bahrain, and the war in Yemen against terrorism. In *Not by the Sword Alone* (2014), Camber Warren observes how 'mass communication technologies allow leaders to convert nationalist images, narratives, and symbols into elements of common knowledge, which are known by all to have been seen by all, and which thereby achieve even greater normative impact'.[72]

Through this manipulative tool, the authoritarian state ensures the creation of an ideal citizen, convinced of the state's democracy by the seriousness of news broadcast by local media outlets. Meanwhile, free speech is restricted, and censorship is a constant threat. Furthermore, self-censorship amongst journalists increases as a result of the dominance of patriotic journalism in the news culture, leading them to deliver biased news to the public with information provided and controlled by the state. This is apparent not only in the media of the Arab Gulf and the Emirates but was also clear in the US press coverage before the invasion of Iraq in 2003, when a number of journalists challenged the Bush administration's claims that Iraq had weapons of mass destruction. Journalist Peter Arnett and talk show host Phil Donahue were fired by the NBC network for their outspoken negative reports and remarks concerning the war.[73]

The rules for correspondents are imposed by the state, in times of stability and crisis, to reinforce the public's loyalty to the leadership and to shape its perception of enemies of the state and the threat those enemies represent to their well-being and safety. These rules restrict journalists' access to accurate information, compelling them to write biased pro-state reports and barring them from speaking openly to avoid dividing public opinion, preventing the public from learning the truth and, more fundamentally, from achieving political maturity.

Today, the effects are exemplified in the Emirates by the pro-state coverage of the war in Yemen, in which declarations such as ones that the UAE 'will continue to fight the global enemy of Al Qaeda' and 'cleanse Yemen of all terror outfits' routinely feature.[74] The consequences can also be seen in the state's attempts to control free expression and suppress public criticism of its handling of political matters, leading, on occasion, to the jailing of academic dissenters and rights activists.[75]

Pro-state press coverage has been demanded from journalists in many places and times to shape public opinion and perceptions of the enemy. In this respect, women have been employed to enhance the state's use of nationalism and patriotism in its propaganda. In *Woman, Nation and State* (1989), Floya Anthias and Nira Yuval-Davis identified five ways in which women participate in national processes:

First, women are constructed as biological reproducers of members of an ethnic group. Second, they are constructed as reproducers of boundaries of ethnic or national groups. Third, they are ideological reproducers of collectivity and transmitters of culture. Fourth, they signify national difference, and therefore, act as symbols in ideological discourse used in the construction, reproduction and transformation of the nation. Finally, women are constructed as participants in national, economic, political and military struggles.[76]

Narratives celebrating Emirati women's emancipation and pride were integrated into the state's patriotic propaganda when the UAE Air Force released images of the country's first female pilot, Major Mariam Al Mansouri, onboard an F-16 fighter ahead of an air strike on ISIS targets in 2014. The images of the groundbreaking pilot, dubbed the 'Pride of the UAE', confirm the state's endorsement of women's emancipation, while it presents itself as both militarily strong and religiously moderate.[77]

In contrast, when women formed feminist movements demanding equality, the patriarchal states of the Middle East and the Arab Gulf specifically viewed them as a threat to religious purity, society, and tradition. Scholars Ilhem Allagui and Abeer Al Najjar argued that

the shift from the representation of idealized women to that of modern women indicates a historical move from private patriarchy, where women are subordinated through their relegation to the home, to public patriarchy, where women are no longer excluded from the public arena, but subordinated within it.[78]

Reactionary responses to Arab women's liberation and feminism remain 'trapped in the hegemonic divisions of modernity; the modern against the traditional, epistemic against political, assimilation against difference'.[79] This is evident in the Islamist and conservative campaigns to Islamise the women's movement and state-backed emancipation projects, efforts that resonate with Nawal El Saadawi's argument that 'Islamic fundamentalist groups are trying to push women *back* to the veil, *back* home, *back* under the domination of their husbands'.[80]

Recently in Kuwait, Safa Al Hashem, the only female member of the 50-seat National Assembly, enraged Islamist and conservative lawmakers when she made critical remarks about a state campaign sponsored by the Ministry of Awqaf (religious endowments) and Islamic Affairs to encourage Kuwaiti women to wear the hijab. Through her account on Twitter, Safa described the campaign, featured in large roadside billboards, 'as strange and unacceptable in a civil country where the constitution guarantees personal freedom', arguing that wearing the hijab is 'a personal decision'.[81] Campaigns such as this project provide a patriarchal, gendered interpretation of how well-mannered women should behave (be obedient) and dress. Similar campaigns to Islamise feminism have spread in Islamic nations outside the Middle East and the Arab Gulf states, like Indonesia, where the Islamist political party Hizbut Tahrir demanded the government to abolish Kartini Day, a national holiday celebrated every year on 21 April as a reminder of Indonesian women's liberation. It was established in 1964 by President Sukarno to celebrate the significant role that educator Raden Adjeng Kartini played in championing Indonesian women's rights. Members of Hizbut Tahrir, however, view her as Westernised and secular and as someone who campaigned for rights that the Islamic law already grants to Indonesian women.[82]

These patriarchal states use Islam as a lens through which to reimagine feminism, yielding Islamic feminism. Iranian feminist lawyer Shirin Ebadi said:

> If Islamic feminism means that a Muslim woman can also be a feminist, and feminism and Islam or Muslimhood does not have to be incompatible, I would agree with it. But if it means that feminism in Muslim societies is somehow peculiar and totally different from feminism in other societies so that it has to be always Islamic, I do not agree with such a concept.[83]

The two-sided coin of the bargain

Looking back at the three key themes discussed in this chapter, it is understandable that the relationship between the Arab Gulf states and women, and women's quest for liberation from the obstacles of patriarchal social norms, is complicated and elicits the following questions: Who are the representatives of patriarchy that women in the Arab Gulf states and in the Emirates, specifically, bargain with, implicitly or explicitly, on a daily basis? Are they family members, bureaucrats, or representatives of the state apparatus? In the Emirati context, the bargain is like a two-sided coin: implicit and explicit, and it is governed by the neopatriarchal leaders of the state, who aim to gradually change gender discourse.

Within the family, the patriarchs resist embracing equality as a concept between women and men in fear of threatening family traditions, reputation, and honour, or the negative consequences of shame—*ayeb*.[84] This forms a gender system that is manifestly kinship-ordered, as described by Valentine Moghadam.[85] In an Emirati context, the gender system not only creates asymmetrical power relations between the sexes but also situates and affects the social processes and social stratification embedded in the construction of the Emirati family. For instance, many Emirati women believe in seeking social emancipation through tribal marriages, rejecting the state feminism effort. To them, gaining knowledge through education may earn them social respect, but in contrast to Western-focused philosophies of gender empowerment, the main mission for Emirati women is to keep their husbands and families rather than pursue personal ambitions and individual growth, as this alone will provide them with a sense of self-worth.

It should be taken into consideration that Emirati women, as much as other Arab Gulf women, share the same set of cultural values as their male counterparts, especially those of maintaining the family's social respectability, preserving the principles of modesty and seclusion of women, and widening the next of kin through the choice of spouse as well as engaging in their kin's private socio-political affairs. Some women would view the state's proposed plans for them with trepidation. As secure as they are within the tenets of their traditional place and power within the family, many women would be unwilling to swap the certainty of their position for an unknown and uncertain situation.[86]

Another group of Emirati women, who constitute the traditional petty bourgeoisie as described by Marxists or belong to the modern salaried middle class,[87] have benefited from state-funded education and emancipation campaigns that have enhanced their status. However, they remain reluctant to voice their concerns publicly in fear of appearing disloyal to the leadership that works to empower them and guarantee their security, particularly their financial security.

Despite having attained academic degrees and entering into professions, modern salaried middle-class Emirati women appear to accept social norms, most importantly social emancipation, as explained previously. They apparently prefer the passive option of preserving the lifestyle and attitudes that their mothers and ancestors passed down to them. And so, to some Emirati women, if not most, submitting to the social norms may not only offer vital social integration, but they may also internalise and believe in these norms, particularly if doing so improves their social status as they grow older.[88]

This acceptance of patriarchal social norms prevents Emirati women from breaking the glass ceiling completely. In a study of the Emirati labour market and women's presence in the public and private sectors, scholar Nick Forster surveyed 337 male and female Emirati employees between February 2008 and June 2011. Emirati women surveyed by Forster revealed reactionary popular sentiments about the state-backed women's empowerment projects. In one case, a 25-year-old female marketing manager said:

> There is still this view that if you're a woman and you have strong opinions that somehow you were not well-raised. So, even if you have a valid opinion about something, some men will either ignore you or think you're some kind of trouble-maker.[89]

The survey also revealed that a third of Emirati men assume that most Emirati women don't have the ability to hold executive positions. And men's concerns extend well beyond doubts about women's professional capacities. As a 38-year-old male manager at a construction company said:

> I do fear the growing power of Emirati women because they may forget our Islamic principles and guidelines, and these women will reflect badly on the image of the UAE as an Islamic country. I believe that it is the responsibility of the man to be the guardian of the woman and to ensure that she does not divert from the right path in any way.[90]

Such notions, which are embedded in Emirati men's and women's minds (just as in Arab men's and women's minds more broadly), convey again the concept of honour (*sharaf*) in tribal patriarchal society.

Apparently, in this game of bargaining, it is the governing leaders of the Emirates who, implicitly and explicitly, play a key role in shifting gender discourse and carry the burden of achieving gradual social change that empowers Emirati women. Supported by rapid economic growth, the leaders have enforced laws to provide the sexes with equal opportunities for education, work, and income and to undermine discrimination and patriarchal social norms. However, their efforts run up against another factor, that of Islam, insofar as UAE laws governing Emirati women's family status, marriage, divorce, inheritance, work, and political practice are religion-based.

As a way forward, the Emirates' leaders have adopted a specific political approach, termed the 'neopatriarchal state'. This involves lobbying the representatives of patriarchal society as well as theologians to promote the Islamic view of the 'complementarity of the sexes'.[91] As described by feminist Freda Hussein, by so doing, they aim to alter the status of Emirati women. In fact, contemporary feminist theologians have used Quranic verses to challenge those who persistently advocate men's superiority over women, such as *Sura Al Baqarah*, verse 2:286, which defines the roles of men and women within a social system equally, regardless of individual capacity. Clearly, in the neopatriarchal state, a term coined by Hisham Sharabi, religion is bound to power and state authority, with the family, rather than the individual, constituting the universal building block of the community. The neopatriarchal state and the patriarchal family reflect and reinforce each other.[92]

To appeal to the patriarchal factions and theologians, even as they sought to enhance the UAE's position as a state in the capitalist world system, the leadership refashioned the position of gender by introducing the notion of gender *balance* rather than equality. In the early 1990s, for instance, the UAE government launched a national project known as Al Asala[93] to promote cultural revival and heritage preservation without sacrificing Islamic values in the name of progress. While the ongoing Al Asala project is based on the revitalisation of indigenous traditions, the UAE government has equated the enhancement of Islamic values with the assertion of Emirati culture. This is evident in a renewed interest in Islamic architecture, the reconstruction of mosques, the establishment of 'heritage areas', and the resurgence of handicraft traditions.[94]

In 2015, the UAE government launched a six-year National Strategy for the Empowerment of Emirati Women. According to the government's website, the strategy's four basic concerns are:

- Maintaining the sustainability of Emirati women's achievements and continuing to achieve further gains;
- Maintaining the social fabric and cohesion through integrating the roles between men and women in order to build a strong and cohesive society able to cope with emerging changes;
- Providing decent and safe social welfare based on high-quality foundations for women; and
- Developing the spirit of responsibility and strengthening the position of Emirati women in regional and international arenas fore.

Significantly, the government's six-year National Strategy for Women has increased their participation in politics, a field that was male dominated even before the country's independence on 2 December 1971. In 2015, women broke the glass ceiling and ran as candidates in national elections for the first time. Eight female candidates were ultimately elected and became members of the National Federal Council, including Dr. Amal Al Qubaisi, who became the first female Speaker of the Assembly to be appointed to the Council.[95] That same year, a federal Gender Balance Council was unveiled. Chaired by Shaikha Manal Bint Mohammad bin Rashid Al Maktoum, daughter of Dubai's ruler, its stated aim is to develop legislation and policy frameworks to narrow the gender gap.

In 2017, Sheikh Mohammed bin Rashid Al Maktoum, UAE's Vice President, Prime Minister, and ruler of Dubai, announced new appointments in a ministerial reshuffle via his official Twitter account. The new cabinet appointments included nine women with an age range of more than half a century, making the UAE cabinet, as journalist James Langton pointed out, considerably more gender-equal than Donald Trump's, which had four women at the time. The appointed female ministers were: Maryam Al Muhairi, Minister of State, responsible for research and planning for the UAE's food security; Sara Al Amiri, Minister of State, responsible for advanced sciences; Hessa Buhumaid, Minister of Community Development;

Oxford graduate Shamma Al Mazroui, Minister of Youth Affairs, who at age 22 became the youngest state minister in the world; Ohood Al Roumi, Minister of State for Happiness; Reem Al Hashimy, Minister of State for International Cooperation; Jameela Al Muhairi, Minister of State for General Education; Dr. Maitha Al Shamsi, Minister of State; and Noura Al Kaabi, Minister of State for Federal National Council Affairs.[96]

Gender balance has become one of the state's political and socio-economic projects. The concept is invoked widely across every media platform to signal an embrace of the global call for equality without ignoring local customs or national identity, which are strongly influenced by the teachings of Islam. With this in mind, the nation's neo-traditionalist or neopatriarchal leadership has developed its own approach to dealing with the issue of gender—that is, by reducing the gender divide. In 2017, the World Economic Forum's Global Gender Gap Report indicated that the Emirates rank second amongst all Arab countries for the sub-index of wage equality for similar work; first for the sub-index of literacy rates amongst women; and first for the sub-index of sex ratio at birth.[97]

To further enhance its global competitiveness in terms of gender balance, the national leadership has been working on another strategy that aims to make the Emirates one of the world's top 25 countries for gender equality by 2021. The leadership's bid to close the gender gap in political empowerment was achieved, as documented in the Global Gender Gap Report released in March 2021.[98] According to recent government studies, Emirati women represent 46.6 percent of the workforce and 66 percent of public sector workers, and 30 percent of them occupy leadership roles. This follows a 2012 government mandate that both government and private organisations employ Emirati women in executive positions and include them in the high-level decision-making process. As a result, Emirati women now run 10 percent of private sector firms.[99]

State Islamic feminism and women's empowerment have been endorsed by the patriarchal, monarchical system in the Emirates to legitimise its nation-building project. Women's associations and emancipation campaigns have been incorporated into the socio-political agenda within specific frameworks, which—even as empowerment efforts proceed—include promoting the view that women have been given all they need and that their essential nature does not permit them to function as full citizens.[100] To release themselves from the confines of patriarchy, Emirati women thus must liberate their collective consciousness from the traditional values that determine their status as second-class citizens, if not utterly inferior. If the liberation of the collective consciousness of Emirati women and Arab women more broadly is achieved, it would place enormous pressure on lawmakers to create gender-equal laws and on Islamic jurists and theologians to produce new exegetical works with a revolutionary outlook—separate from secular epistemology and mirroring the truth of Islam as a moderate religion, which is evident in Quranic verses that champion equality for men and women in education, civil and legal rights, and the basic human right of free expression.

Conclusion

Media, as an industry and a profession, was not built on a strong foundation when the Emiratis formed a nation 50 years ago. The resources were limited due to the lack of technology, education, and understanding of the overall role of media in creating a diverse and intellectual community that not only receives news in the form of print or broadcast but also analyses it to deliver opinions from a variety of perspectives.

This study thus presents an in-depth examination of media development, the emergence of women's journalism in the Emirates, and the particular socio-cultural challenges that female journalists encounter in tribal, patriarchal society. In fact, Emirati women in this field were virtually invisible until the 1970s, when a few of them decided to take a daring step into what was a male-dominated field by writing features for newspapers, entering the newsroom as editors or television hosts, and obtaining scholarships to study media and mass communication in neighbouring Arab countries.

The early wave of female Emirati journalists (1970s–1990s) faced unceasing criticism for defying the patriarchal system by choosing media as an academic degree and profession rather than degrees and employment in fields labelled re-spectable for women, such as nursing and education. The next wave of Emirati female journalists (2000s to the present), however, were exposed to a different range of challenges by the local media corporations, which distinguish between journalists on the basis of gender and do not provide women with an appropri-ate work environment or opportunities for growth. Another challenge is posed by the media regulators (the National Media Council), whose regulations have limited the practice of investigative journalism, which has turned the younger generation of Emiratis and media graduates away from this field.

Beside the challenging conditions of employment in the media industry, which include long work hours, fairly low salaries, and overtly misogynistic chief edi-tors, which are analysed in Chapters 4, 5, and 6, there is an enormous chasm be-tween what Emirati media graduates have studied and what they then encounter once working professionally in the Emirates. Most of the academic curricula and modules reflect best practice in the media from a Western perspective, which dif-fers greatly from the reality of media practice in the Arab world.[101]

Many Emirati media graduates, as a result, avoid joining the media industry, preferring to apply their university-taught journalistic skills in institutional jobs such as government press officers, which provide better opportunities for promo-tion and financial benefits. The social mores of respect and honour that Emirati society values also often stand against the practice of investigative journalism, de-terring Emiratis, men and women alike, from pursuing careers in the profession and steering them into different industries.[102]

Emirati women's relative absence in the fields of print and broadcast media and in analysing political and economic news stories has been widely observed. Women do, however, have a limited media presence, covering social issues such as healthcare, childcare, education, fashion, and lifestyle. To examine this field, I have conducted one-on-one interviews with 40 Emirati and Arab expat journalists, divided into two groups of 30 Emirati and Arab expat women and ten Emirati and Arab expat men, to obtain different perspectives on gender identity and dynamics, on socio-cultural constraints, and on stereotypes affecting this field. In these semi-structured interviews, interviewees have been categorised based on generational cohort: Emirati and Arab expat journalists from the early generation (1970s–1990s) and Emirati and Arab expat journalists from the new generation (2000s–onward). In addition, participant observation has been used to observe Emirati male and fe-male journalists' routines and activities inside the newsroom for a duration of four weeks, divided into two weeks each. This took place at Dubai TV and Abu Dhabi Channel One, which belong to two major local media corporations: Dubai Media Incorporated, located in the Emirate of Dubai, and Abu Dhabi Media Company, located in the Emirate of Abu Dhabi.

By applying these methods, this study aims to identify the social and cultural factors that challenge Emirati female journalists and, in particular, the impact of gender identity on their presence in this field, which has often been defined as an issue of human resources or organisational diversity. It also aims to identify the factors that have made journalism an undesirable job for Emirati women and pre-sent practical measures to tackle these challenges. These include nationalising the media corporations to increase the number of employed Emirati female journalists, which could be achieved by developing specific academic and training schemes to help them enhance their professional skills, better understand the requirements of the industry, and gain expertise from renowned regional and international media academies and experts in print and broadcast media.

With this context in mind, this study addresses four key issues: the socio-cultural factors that challenge Emirati female journalists, the glass ceiling that Emirati female journalists face in their professional careers, the impact of the 'gen-dered' masculine culture of the newsroom on journalistic practices and norms in the Emirates, and the impact of gender inequality on Emirati female journalists' presence in this field.

Notes

1 Herb (1999, pp. 53–54).
2 Ibid., p. 56.
3 Those of *khadiri* status include people whose ancestors came from other, non-Arab places in the Middle East, whose ancestors were expelled from tribes and forced to take up unseemly occupations out of economic necessity (Herb, 1999, pp. 53–55).
4 It is estimated that there are 100,000 stateless people in the Emirates who migrated from Iran, lost their legal documents during the sea voyage, and settled in before the federal union of the seven emirates or sheikhdoms in 1971 (Ghazal, 2008).
5 Davidson (2013, p. 137).
6 Ghazal (2008).
7 Herb (1999, p. 16).
8 Stockmann (2013, p. 28).
9 Sakr (2004, p. 11).

10 Ibid., p. 9.
11 Allagui and Al Najjar (2018, p. 70).
12 Walby (1991, pp. 19, 20).
13 Ibid., p. 21.
14 Ibid., p. 20.
15 Ibid., p. 21.
16 Ibid.
17 Ibid.
18 Sikoska (1999, p. 2).
19 Ibid.
20 N'Guessan (2011, p. 187).
21 Jenks (2003, p. 28).
22 Ibid.
23 Ibid.
24 Bartky (1990, p. 25).
25 Lerner (1986, p. 43).
26 Ibid., p. 86.
27 Ibid.
28 De Beauvoir (2011, p. 5).
29 Lerner (1986, p. 44).
30 Bourdieu (2001, p. 26).
31 An Arabic word with multiple connotations. From a political perspective, it means trial and war. From a sexual perspective, it means seduction and temptation.
32 Arabic for forbidden or prohibited acts, objects, or conducts.
33 N'Guessan (2011, p. 187).
34 Marron glacé is a French dessert of candied chestnuts. The sobriquet was used by opponents of Doria Shafiq in mockery, referring to her appearance at the expense of her intelligence.
35 Massoud (2010).
36 Sadiqi (2016, p. 247).
37 Tribal inhabitants occupied this land (the Emirates today) for about 7,500 years, dating back to 5000 BCE, and were dependent on pastoralism, pearl diving, fishing, and hunting in the eastern mountains (Al Abed and Hellyer, 2001, pp. 7–28).
38 Metz (1994, p. 37).
39 Peterson (1977, p. 2).
40 Efforts to preach the Bible, in particular, were unsuccessful due to the lack of education and modern school facilities, as well as the difficulty of teaching the English language to the locals, who showed no interest. Therefore, foreign missionaries offered medical care and taught young women basic handcrafts to sell in the marketplace (Sonbol, 2012, p. 242).
41 Sonbol (2012, p. 242).
42 Hawker (2013, p. 5).
43 Soffan (1980, p. 18).
44 Al Malki et al. (2012, p. 112).
45 Soffan (1980, p. 16).
46 Ibid., p. 23.
47 Milani (2011, p. 64).
48 Mernissi (1975, p. 10).
49 Ibid., p. 15.
50 A hybrid of Wahabism and conservative Islam, Salafism is a revivalist movement established by Sunni theologians between the 1970s and 1980s and is still widespread in the Arab Gulf states.
51 A revivalist movement formed by Sunni theologians in pursuit of Islamic purity.

52 Peck (2008, p. 314).
53 The chain of narrators attesting to the historical authenticity of a particular hadith or the prophetical quotes.
54 Ftouni (2012, p. 165).
55 Ftouni (2012).
56 Peterson (1977, p. 297).
57 Sadig (2019).
58 Arabic for 'courts' or 'reception halls'.
59 Al Awazem is an influential Bedouin tribe long allied with the Al Sabah ruling family in Kuwait (Sabah, 2013, p. 98).
60 Bartky (1990, p. 22).
61 Ibid., p. 23.
62 Doumato and Posusney (2003).
63 N'Guessan (2011, p. 193).
64 Rahbani (2010, p. 94).
65 Franks (2013, p. 26).
66 Chambers et al. (2004, p. 91).
67 Reporters Without Borders (2021).
68 Davidson (2013, p. 146).
69 Ibid., p. 148.
70 Ibid., p. 149.
71 Ibid., p. 148.
72 Pomeroy, 2017, pp. 14–15.
73 Ibid., p. 19.
74 Trew (2018).
75 Most of these academic dissenters and right activists were influenced by the Muslim Brotherhood ideology and planned to overthrow legitimate governments in the GCC as an aftermath of the Arab Spring.
76 Sakr (2004, pp. 72–73).
77 Allagui and Al Najjar (2018, p. 76).
78 Ibid., pp. 73–74.
79 Ftouni (2012, p. 163).
80 Sakr (2004, p. 83).
81 Izzak (2018).
82 Muttaqin (2018).
83 Ruether (2007, p. 105).
84 Arabic for 'shame'. In the study of superego development, it refers to the cultivation of conformity and fear of others' criticism rather than individualism and self-criticism (Broucek, 1991, p. 8).
85 Moghadam (2003, p. 15).
86 Pinto (2012).
87 Moghadam (2003).
88 Jütting (2007, p. 60).
89 Forster (2017, p. 109).
90 Ibid., p. 99.
91 Moghadam (2003, p. 7).
92 Ibid., p. 11.
93 Arabic for 'cultural authenticity'.
94 Pinto (2012).
95 Dajani (2015).
96 Day (2018).
97 UAE Government (2017).
98 World Economic Forum (2021, p. 26).
99 Day (2018).

100 Krause (2009, p. 65).
101 On 25 May 1981, the Arabian Peninsula states formed an intergovernmental union and inaugurated the Gulf Cooperation Council (GCC), commonly referred to as 'the Gulf states'.
102 Al Subaihi (2012).

References

Al Abed, I. and Hellyer, P. (2001). *United Arab Emirates: A New Perspective*. Abu Dhabi: Trident Press.
Al Malki, A., Kaufer, D., Ishizaki, S. and Dreher, K. (2012). *Arab Women in Arab News*. New York, NY: Bloomsbury Publishing.
Al Murr, H. E. (1998). The Wink of the Mona Lisa and Other Stories from the Gulf. Translated by Jack Briggs. Dubai: Motivate Publishing. (Original work published 1994.)
Al Subaihi, T. (2012). 'As the Nation Races Ahead, the Media Needs More Emiratis'. *The National*. 4 March. Available at: https://www.thenational.ae/as-the-nation-races-ahead-the-media-needs-more-emiratis-1.364370 [Accessed 18 September 2017].
Allagui, I. and Al Najjar, A. (2018). 'From Women Empowerment to Nation Branding: A Case Study from the United Arab Emirates'. *International Journal of Communication*, 12, pp. 68–85.
Bartky, S. (1990). *Femininity and Domination: Studies in the Phenomenology of Oppression*. New York, NY: Routledge.
Bourdieu, P. (2001). *Masculine Domination*. Stanford, UK: Stanford University Press.
Broucek, F. (1991). *Shame and the Self*. New York, NY: Guilford Press.
Chambers, D., Steiner, L. and Fleming, C. (2004). *Women and Journalism*. London: Routledge.
Dajani, H. (2015). 'UAE News in Review 2015: FNC Elections Break Glass Ceiling'. *The National*. 30 December. Available at: https://www.thenational.ae/uae/government/uae-news-in-review-2015-fnc-elections-break-glass-ceiling-1.111055 [Accessed 31 August 2018].
Davidson, C. (2013). *After the Sheikhs: The Coming Collapse of the Gulf Monarchies*. Oxford: Oxford University Press.
Day, E. (2018). 'Meet the Nine Female Ministers in the UAE's Current Cabinet'. *Emirates Woman*. 15 February. Available at: http://emirateswoman.com/meet-the-nine-female-ministers-in-the-uaes-current-cabinet/ [Accessed 31 August 2018].
De Beauvoir, S. (2011). *The Second Sex*. London: Vintage.
Doumato, E. and Posusney, M. (2003). *Women and Globalization in the Arab Middle East*. Boulder, CO: Rienner.
Downing, N. E. and Roush, K. L. (1985). 'From Passive Acceptance to Active Commitment: A Model of Feminist Identity Development for Women', *The Counseling Psychologist*. 13(4), pp. 695–709. https://doi.org/10.1177/0011000085134013
Forster, N. (2017). *A Quiet Revolution: The Rise of Women Managers, Business Owners and Leaders in the Arabian Gulf States*. Cambridge, UK: Cambridge University Press.
Franks, S. (2013). *Women and Journalism*. London: I.B. Tauris.
Ftouni, L. (2012). 'Rethinking Gender Studies: Towards an Arab Feminist Epistemology', in T. Sabry (ed.) *Arab Cultural Studies: Mapping the Field*. London: I.B. Tauris & Co Ltd.
Ghazal, R. (2008). 'The Frustration of Being a Bidoon'. *The National*. 6 November. Available at: https://www.thenational.ae/uae/the-frustration-of-being-a-bidoon-1.505830 [Accessed 7 July 2020].
Hawker, R. (2013). 'Imagining a Bedouin Past: Stereotypes and Cultural Representation in the Contemporary United Arab Emirates'. *Semantic Scholar*. January. Available at: https://pdfs.semanticscholar.org/2199/cdf7694bb3cfc4a4f24b072ead6fca93487e.pdf [Accessed 7 May 2018].

Herb, M. (1999). *All in the Family*. Albany: State University of New York Press.

Human Rights Watch. (2009). 'UAE: Media Law Undermines Free Expression. Vague Content Restrictions, Strict Controls Hamper Independence of Press'. 13 April. Available at: https://www.hrw.org/news/2009/04/13/uae-media-law-undermines-free-expression [Accessed 14 May 2022].

Izzak, B. (2018). 'MP Al Hashem Remarks on Hijab Triggers Controversy'. *Kuwait Times*. 12 April. Available at: http://news.kuwaittimes.net/website/mp-al-hashem-remarks-on-hijab-triggers-controversy [Accessed 28 September 2018].

Jenks, C. (2003). *Culture*. 2nd edn. London, UK: Routledge.

Jütting, J. (2007). *Development Centre Studies Informal Institutions: How Social Norms Help or Hinder Development*. Ukraine: OECD Publishing.

Khatib, L. (2004). 'The Orient and Its Others: Women as Tools of Nationalism in Egyptian Political Cinema', in N. Sakr (ed.) *Women and Media in the Middle East: Power through Self-Expression, pp. 72–88*. New York, NY: I.B. Tauris & Co Ltd.

Krause, W. (2009). 'Gender and Participation in the Arab Gulf'. *London School of Economics Research Online*. September. Available at: http://eprints.lse.ac.uk/55255/1/Krause_2009.pdf [Accessed 8 May 2019].

Lerner, G. (1986). *The Creation of Patriarchy*. Oxford, UK: Oxford University Press.

Massoud, E. (2010). 'Doria Shafik: A Woman Who Struggled for Women, Then Took Her Own Life Because She Was a Woman'. *Al Gamal*. 22 March. Translated by the author. Available at: https://www.algamal.net/7126 [Accessed 17 June 2017].

Metz, H. (1994). *Persian Gulf States*. Washington, DC: Federal Research Division, Library of Congress.

Mernissi, F. (1975). *Beyond the veil: Male-Female Dynamics in Modern Muslim Society*. Cambridge, MA: Schenkman Publishing Company.

Milani, F. (2011). *Words, Not Swords: Iranian Women Writers and the Freedom of Movement*. Syracuse, NY: Syracuse University Press.

Moghadam, V. (2003). *Modernizing Women: Gender and Social Change in the Middle East*. Boulder, CO: L. Rienner.

Muttaqin, F. (2018). 'Islamization of Women's Movement in Indonesia'. *The Jakarta Post*. 20 April. Available at: http://www.thejakartapost.com/academia/2018/04/20/islamization-of-womens-movement-in-indonesia.html [Accessed 29 September 2018].

N'Guessan, K. (2011). 'Gender Hierarchy and the Social Construction of Femininity: The Imposed Mask'. *Semantic Scholar*. September. Available at: https://pdfs.semanticscholar.org/6c2d/b6bb01b97a6f15b4d88aebe9d5294fd49efa.pdf [Accessed 15 July 2018].

Peck, M. (2008). *Historical Dictionary of the Gulf Arab States*. 2nd edn. Lanham, MD: Scarecrow Press.

Peterson, J. E. (1977). 'Tribes and Politics in Eastern Arabia'. *Middle East Journal*, 31(3), pp. 297–312.

Pinto, V. C. (2012). *Nation-Building, State and the Genderframing of Women's Rights in the United Arab Emirates (1971-2009)*. 1st edn. London: Garnet Publishing, Limited.

Pomeroy, B. (2017). 'Mediated Nationalism: Press Freedom, Mass Media, and Nationalism'. *Dudley Knox Library*. Calhoun Institutional Archive of the Naval Postgraduate School. December. Available at: https://calhoun.nps.edu/bitstream/handle/10945/56785/17Dec_Pomeroy_Brenton.pdf?sequence=1&isAllowed=y [Accessed 24 July 2018].

Rahbani, L. (2010). 'Women in Arab Media: Present but Not Heard'. *I Know Politics*. 16 February. Available at: http://iknowpolitics.org/sites/default/files/leila20nicolas20rahbaniarab20women20in20the20media.pdf [Accessed 9 July 2019].

Reporters Without Borders. (2021). *2021 World Press Freedom Index*. Available at: https://rsf.org/en/2021-world-press-freedom-index-journalism-vaccine-against-disinformation-blocked-more-130-countries [Accessed 4 August 2022].

Ruether, R. (2007). *Feminist Theologies*. Minneapolis, MN: Fortress Press.

Sabah, M. (2013). *Gender and Politics in Kuwait: Women and Political Participation in the Gulf*. London: Tauris.

Sadig, H. (2019). *Al Jazeera in the Gulf and in the World*. Singapore: Palgrave Macmillan.

Sadiqi, F. (2016). *Women's Movements in Post–'Arab Spring' North Africa*. New York, NY: Palgrave Macmillan.

Sakr, N. (ed.). (2004). *Women and Media in the Middle East: Power through Self-Expression*. New York, NY: I.B. Tauris & Co Ltd.

Sikoska, T. (1999). 'Introducing Gender in Conflict and Conflict Prevention: Conceptual and Policy Implications'. *Norman Patterson School of International Relations*. Santo Domingo. United Nations International Research and Training Institute for the Advancement of Women. 16 December. Available at: https://www.peacewomen.org/sites/default/files/un-instraw_genderconflictprevpolicy_1999_0.pdf [Accessed 8 July 2017].

Soffan, L. (1980). *Women of the United Arab Emirates*. London: Croom Helm Ltd.

Sonbol, A. (2012). *Gulf Women*. Doha: Bloomsbury Qatar Foundation Publications.

Stockmann, D. (2013). *Media Commercialization and Authoritarian Rule in China*. Cambridge: Cambridge University Press.

Trew, B. (2018). 'A Revealing Look Inside the UAE's War on Al-Qaeda in Yemen'. *The Independent*. 15 August. Available at: https://www.independent.co.uk/news/world/middle-east/uae-yemen-civil-war-al-qaeda-aden-dar-saad-gulf-saudi-arabia-conflict-a8492021.html [Accessed 28 July 2018].

UAE Government. (2017). *Gender Balance*. Official Portal of the UAE Government. Available at: https://www.government.ae/en/information-and-services/social-affairs/women [Accessed 31 August 2018].

Walby, S. (1991). *Theorizing Patriarchy*. Oxford, UK: Basil Blackwell.

Warren, T. C. (2014). 'Not by the Sword Alone: Soft Power, Mass Media, and the Production of State Sovereignty'. *International organization*, 68(1), pp. 111–141.

World Economic Forum. (2021). *Global Gender Gap Report 2021*. Available at: https://www.weforum.org/publications/global-gender-gap-report-2021 [Accessed 8 February 2024].

Yuval-Davis, N., Anthias, F. and Campling, J. (1989). *Woman, nation, state*. Houndmills, Basingstoke, Hampshire: Macmillan.

3   Ethnography in the Newsroom

There is a dearth of feminist media studies focused on Arab Gulf states, and the issue of gender within the media industry, in particular, is greatly underexamined. Gender equality, as a modern Western ideal, has no foundation in the culture of the Arab Gulf states, except in Islamic law, or *sharia*, which mentions men's and women's rights when it comes to education and the ownership of businesses, for example. As discussed in Chapter 2, Emirati women live in a tribal patriarchal society and have only limited responsibilities outside the domestic realm, with little or no authority in economic and social affairs, despite several state initiatives to champion Emirati women's emancipation in the workplace. Gender came to the fore in the Emirates in 2002 after the publication of the United Nations report that revealed the low proportion of Emirati women involved in political decision-making.[1] However, according to scholar Suaad Al Oraimi, Emirati culture has 'still not developed a fixed mechanism for dealing with' the concept of gender, which 'requires feminist intellectual unity, based on belief in the unity of women's identity, and this does not exist in the UAE'.[2]

Like gender, feminism is alien to the Arab Gulf and Emirati societies, but both concepts have become part of state modernisation efforts and state-sponsored initiatives to update the traditional role of women and empower them. In a 2009 study on gender and participation in the Arab Gulf, scholar Wanda Krause argues that these initiatives, while expanding Arab Gulf women's independence and empowerment to some extent, will not alter the status of gender as a concept in the region. Krause explains:

> Women of these nations are typically prohibited from criticizing their government. Within the UAE, the government either runs women's organizations, or sponsors the running of women's organizations. Therefore, involvement in such groups referred to as either government-run organizations or government-organized non-government organizations, leads women toward following the policies of the state.[3]

As noted in the introduction, a few studies on the development of the media in the Emirates from a historical perspective have been published; following Ezzat's *Al Sihafa Fi Dowal Al Khaleej Al Arabi* and Nafadi's *Al Sihafa Fi Dowlat*

DOI: 10.4324/9781003488415-3

Al Emarat Al Arabiya, there was Emirati academic Alia Hassan's *Our Media Identity* (2011). A few academics have published studies that offer some limited insight into media culture and law in the Emirates, such as William Rugh, whose *Arab Mass Media: Newspapers, Radio, and Television in Arab Politics* (2004) has a chapter on Emirati media; and Adnan Jasim BuMetea, with *Political Communication in the Arabian Gulf Countries* (2013). In addition to *Media Law in the United Arab Emirates*, Matt J. Duffy wrote an article, 'Cultures of Journalism in Arabic and English-Language Newspapers Within the United Arab Emirates' (2013), that analyses the content of two daily newspapers, the Arabic *Al Ittihad* and the English-language *The National*, founded in 2008. Duffy, who taught international media law at the College of Communications and Media Sciences at Zayed University for two years, was eventually deported due to his frank approach to teaching media law and ethics.[4] His book on Emirati media law and its analysis of the complex legal issues surrounding censorship practices has been significant to this study.

To gain a deep understanding of media development and culture in the Emirates, I investigated three areas that have been underexamined: self-censorship practices in the newsroom, gender dynamics and the attitudes about gender roles experienced by female journalists, and the link between patriarchy and the empowerment of female journalists in the Emirates. My main methodology includes (1) participant observation recorded in diary entries to provide the reader with a vivid picture of everyday journalistic practices that I observed in the newsrooms and (2) semi-structured interviews.

Using these two interrelated qualitative approaches, I gathered a substantial amount of evidence that has provided a deeper picture of the complexity surrounding gender dynamics and their association with the social constructs of Emirati tribal society. I have also analysed the influence of these social constructs on the media landscape in the Emirates, which is seen as patriotic and loyal to the state. The observations and interviews illuminate how gender and authoritarianism dictate journalistic practices and routines in the newsroom, where *a priori* censorship is commonplace and barriers are created to limit Emirati female journalists' progress in the field.

Participant observation

The use of participant observation, in which ethnographers engage in fieldwork to observe people's habits and schemes, bearing in mind their cultural differences, has been widespread in Western media studies. According to anthropologist Clifford Geertz, participant observation provides a 'thick description of a culture or group' and calls on 'researchers [to] consider the relevant social context, which helps them to understand that their observations are representations of a group's cultural reality'.[5] The use of participant observation as an ethnographic approach in media studies began in the 1930s when three American scholars from the Chicago School of Urban Ethnography developed guiding principles for students to use in their research. Robert Park, W. I. Thomas, and

Ernest Burgess observed the similarities in ethnographic and journalistic work and encouraged ethnographers to employ journalistic methods.[6] The participant observation method was taken up by other researchers to examine media practices, such as Philip Schlesinger, who investigated British news production in 1978; Philip Elliot, who observed a television production team for a British documentary programme for four months in 1972; and Tom Burns, who undertook an extensive study of media organisations and bureaucracy by observing journalists at the BBC in 1977.[7]

For this study, my aim was to use participant observation in the form of diary entries to understand the socio-cultural factors that shape the lives of Emirati and Arab expat journalists, their thoughts and beliefs about the media environment in the Emirates, and their opinions on the outdated media law to shed light on newsroom culture and practices in the Emirates. To conduct this study, I took on the role of observer-as-participant. The observer-as-participant methodology requires ethnographers to reveal their identity while engaged in fieldwork but to limit their encounters and engagement with the people being observed.[8] In addition, researchers who take on the role of observer-as-participant document their observations using field notes to record what they have seen, instead of what they have experienced, while observing people's attitudes and activities.[9]

I intended to undertake participant observation in three popular news centres in the Emirates: Dubai News Centre, operated by Dubai Media Incorporated; Sharjah News Centre, operated by Sharjah Media Centre; and Abu Dhabi News Centre, operated by Abu Dhabi Media Company. However, the process of contacting official representatives at these news centres was difficult and perplexing. It took four months, from October 2016 to January 2017, of long-distance calls and emails from London to convince the representatives of the study's importance, and to receive approval for access to the newsrooms. Long before starting this fieldwork journey, I had repeatedly heard from relatives, friends, and academics some version of the phrase '*Wasta*[10] is your access ticket'—it was widely believed that having an influential figure intervene on my behalf would grant me immediate access to resources, along with other privileges; I declined the ticket. Eventually, I received approval from the Dubai News Centre, followed by the Abu Dhabi News Centre. Sharjah News Centre never responded at all, despite my attempts to follow up by phone and email.

After the approvals were provisionally granted, I was asked to submit official letters from my supervisor and the university, to draft a fact sheet in Arabic about the study, and to attend brief meetings to further discuss the plan and timeline of the fieldwork with officers of the news centres, including their general directors. During these meetings, I noticed that there was a level of hesitation about my observing the newsroom and how my observations might be documented, because the concept of gender equality, for instance, has no basis in Emirati society, while the concepts of press freedom and censorship are considered too sensitive to be discussed openly.

At the end of the meetings, I was advised by the director generals for both centres to spend three hours inside the newsroom starting at 6 pm when most of the editorial staff would be present, and witness for myself the work routine and production of news before the daily broadcast of the one-hour local evening news, which aired starting at 8 pm from what both newsrooms referred to as 'the Gallery'.[11] The on-air sequencing of the stories is strictly hierarchical, with each broadcast leading with the national news, starting with official pronouncements from the executive branch of the government—the president, then the vice president, then cabinet ministers, and so forth. Following that, Dubai TV's *Akhbar Al Emarat* (Emirates news) highlights news related to the federal emirate of Dubai, while Abu Dhabi TV's *Oloum Al Dar*[12] focuses on the capital city of Abu Dhabi.

In addition, the director generals for both news centres barred me from attending the editorial meetings to avoid my documenting confidential communication. When I stated that I needed to observe the pre-rundown meeting at the beginning of the week and the retrospective meeting at the end of the week to analyse the editorial team's viewpoints on news planning and production, my request was denied. The director general explained that it was unnecessary for me to observe these meetings as broadcast plans often shift during the editing process, especially if an urgent news story comes in. They added that the editorial teams at both newsrooms use the WhatsApp platform and other applications to assign tasks, answer inquiries, and inform colleagues about medical absences, meaning that each week there was either just one full team meeting—held on Mondays, in the case of the Dubai newsroom—or none at all, in the case of the Abu Dhabi newsroom.

The scepticism about more presence was even more evident when I observed the day-to-day routine of Emirati and Arab expat journalists from a desk allocated to me within the respective newsrooms, in three-hour slots from 6 to 9 pm, for 14 days, excluding Fridays and Saturdays. For instance, during my first few days of observation inside the Dubai newsroom, Emirati journalists and senior editors in the vicinity would speak in low tones to avoid their conversations being documented and would often explicitly tell me that our exchanges were not to be written down in my field notes. However, some Emirati journalists and editors, especially those who held academic degrees in mass communication, would often ask about ethnography, which was new to them, as they were acquainted only with quantitative research methodologies such as surveys and questionnaires. This gave me an opportunity to engage in conversations with Emirati journalists, in particular, who were confident enough to talk openly about newsroom practices and certain taboo subjects that cannot be broadcast in the Emirati media.

Besides this, I aimed to observe the activities and tasks assigned to each team member, to analyse the conversations inside the two newsrooms, and to study body language for any signs of gendered attitudes towards female journalists in particular. There was also an opportunity to examine the activities and tasks assigned to team members broadcasting local news for Dubai One,[13] an

English-language subchannel created by Dubai Media Incorporated in 2004. *Dubai One News*, which broadcasts local, sports, and economic news segments, was hosted by Emirati and foreign expat anchors. I briefly observed them as they used the same studio facilities as *Akhbar Al Emarat*, though the two editorial teams had little interaction. Observing the live broadcast of *Dubai One News* gave me an insight into English-language TV news production in the Emirates, which follows the same hierarchical format.[14]

Semi-structured interviews

In a semi-structured interview process, a researcher conducts recorded interviews to collect evidence and statements on people's stories. In Western media studies, specifically, the use of semi-structured interviews as a qualitative method began in the 1960s to chronicle the histories of major newspapers and corporations, as well as the biographies of prominent media founders and owners.[15]

For this study, I conducted one-to-one interviews with 40 Emirati and Arab expat journalists, aiming to record their testimonies and experiences in practising journalism and their perspectives on the newsroom culture and media environment in the Emirates. The only previous study to examine the political system and the press in the Emirates using semi-structured interviews was conducted by A. Rashed, who interviewed the editors of three local Arabic dailies in 1995 for a master's thesis, 'The Relationship between the Press and Political Authority in the UAE: Applied Study on Al Etihad, Al Bayan, and Al Etihad Newspapers from 1972 to 1990'.[16]

For the present study, the interviewed journalists represented the following local print and broadcast media outlets:

1 Abu Dhabi Television Channel One
2 Emirates News Agency (WAM)
3 *Al Ittihad* daily newspaper (Abu Dhabi)
4 *Al Bayan* daily newspaper (Dubai)
5 *Al Khaleej* daily newspaper (Sharjah)
6 *Al Roeya* daily newspaper (Abu Dhabi)
7 *Zahrat Al Khaleej* women's weekly magazine (Abu Dhabi)
8 *Al Azminah Al Arabiya* weekly magazine (Sharjah)
9 *Awraq* weekly magazine (Sharjah)

The interviewees came from different schools of thought, influenced by their culture, education, and previous experiences in journalism in other Arab countries. Amongst the ten male journalists, there were six Arab expats who came from Egypt (four) and Palestine (two), each with more than 20 years of experience, and who all expressed concerns about the oppressive media environment in the Emirates. The remaining four male journalists were Emiratis, who were born between the 1950s and 1970s and have had a relatively positive experience in journalism. As for the 30 female journalists, the lengths of their careers spanned from 2 to 30 years. Twenty-one were Emiratis, while the remaining nine came from Jordan, Morocco, Syria, Egypt, and Iraq. Their testimonies revealed the hardships they experienced working in a male-controlled, male-dominated industry, let alone working in countries like Iraq, where the media systems were controlled by dictatorships. Alongside their accounts of inequality and harassment in the newsroom, they also expressed their aspirations for a better media environment that gives them empowerment through expression.

The one-to-one interviews started on 15 February 2017 and ended on 1 May 2017. I managed to contact, by phone and email, personal assistants and meet with editors-in-chief at the targeted local media outlets through acquaintances with whom I worked closely during my nine-year tenure as a PR professional and former university classmates who have become successful media professionals. Responding to explanations of the importance of the study in documenting the history of media development in the Emirates, editors-in-chief welcomed my requests to conduct the interviews and allowed me to speak freely with their journalists to schedule mutually convenient interview dates. All 40 interviews took place in private meeting rooms inside the newsrooms, and each journalist signed a consent form approving the publication of their testimony.

Notably, two large local media corporations that produce top English-speaking dailies did not allow me access to interview their journalists. When I visited the head offices of both *The National*[17] and *Gulf News*,[18] I was escorted to their respective HR departments, where representatives were keen on viewing the list of questions rather than learning about the study. At *The National's* head office, for instance, the HR manager, an Egyptian woman, contacted the editor-in-chief. Judging from the HR manager's facial expression and the hushed tone of their conversation, I understood immediately that accessibility to the newsroom was impossible. When I asked for an explanation, the manager told me that *The National's* journalists are not allowed to meet with researchers in adherence with the newspaper's HR policy. At *Gulf News*, the scenario was different. The HR representatives, two Indians, were openly against the idea of my meeting the newspaper's Emirati editor-in-chief and seemed intimidated by the prospect of their journalists answering questions that could potentially involve voicing opinions on the topics of self-censorship and the oppressive media law in the Emirates. I understood their concern and their possible fear of losing their jobs if they were to permit *Gulf News'* journalists to participate, and thus I was not insistent.

I engaged in standardised, semi-structured interviews with all interviewees, asking identical questions of each in the same sequence.[19] The list of interview questions I prepared aimed to document their personal stories and determine the socio-cultural factors that contribute to gender inequality in Emirati media.

Some questions alarmed the chosen journalists as they addressed notions of gender politics that are often unvoiced inside the newsroom, particularly amongst female journalists regardless of age and nationality. For example, when I asked the interviewees if they thought that journalism as a profession was gendered, I received different opinions that made it clear that gender as a concept was widely misunderstood. Male journalists, specifically, thought that the word 'gendered' was exclusively associated with the issue of gender equality, a matter of concern, as they saw it, only to women and feminists. Emirati male journalists, especially, overestimated Emirati women's representation in leadership positions in every vital sector, including politics, as a result of the governing leadership's empowerment campaigns. These participants were neglecting the reality that gender inequality exists in the Emirates as much as in other parts of the Arab world, due to patriarchy and societal norms that impose gender restrictions on men and women alike. Some female journalists misunderstood the same question, thinking that the word 'gendered' referred only to the predominance of men. Those who were aware of gender-related issues, however, gave elaborate answers narrating their experience of gender stereotypes and gender discrimination in the workplace as well as at home, where they grew up learning that gender restriction is a social norm.[20]

The interview questions covered other topics crucial to this study, including the practice of self-censorship and the newsroom culture in the Emirates. For example, the participants were asked if they faced any resistance in terms of content or whether stories they drafted had been banned from publication. When asked if they felt threatened by the media law or the media authorities, some journalists refused to comment on their experiences with the censors, who represent the media authorities in the Emirates. Others openly described how the practice of self-censorship saved them from court battles and legal punishment, which had resulted in the closing down of several local dailies.

Because the nature of the interview questions sparked astonishing revelations and eye-opening narratives about the journalists' experiences, some of them preferred to be anonymous and accordingly signed the consent form I created using pseudonyms or fictitious names to hide their true identities. Eight female journalists used pseudonyms, while one male journalist did so. The reason for this, as they told me, was the fear of their revelations and accusations becoming known by colleagues and executives, particularly by those who perpetrated mistreatment against them by practising gender politics inside the newsroom. In addition, the anonymity provided these nine journalists with a sense of assurance and confidence to criticise the practice of censorship and the punishing terms of the media law. The other journalists, however, who wished to have their true identities revealed were not intimidated by the interview questions, which they answered expressly motivated by the belief that the ongoing battle of sexes inside the newsroom must be investigated and resolved by the implementation of policies to secure journalists' rights to free speech and end gender inequality.

The semi-structured interviews, which were voice-recorded with the interviewees' consent,[21] were conducted with journalists who were categorised based on the following:

1 Gender: 30 female journalists and ten male journalists
2 Stratification: journalists from the early generation (1970s–1990s), between the ages of 30 and 60, and journalists from the new generation (2000s–onward), in their 20s

   The reason behind selecting interviewees based on gender and stratification was to determine how gender dynamics and gender inequality in the newsroom had emerged and developed between two generations in the Emirates and the different experiences of inequality by the two generations. In a 1968 study on intergenerational transmission, sociologist Otis Duncan defined 'social stratification' as 'the persistence of positions in a hierarchy of inequality, either over the lifetime of a birth cohort of individuals, or more particularly, between generations'.[22] In the course of the semi-structured interviews, a number of the participants were hesitant about having their age listed,[23] especially women who confided in me that they were close to the legal retirement age. Some others shyly preferred to keep this detail discreet, a request that I respected out of decorum. Amongst the chosen male journalists, however, only one interviewee avoided listing his age, explaining that he has often been viewed as too young to hold the position of editor-in-chief for a daily newspaper that is funded by the government.

Notes

 1 The UAE ranks 105 out of 128 countries for gender equality, according to the 2007 Global Gender Gap Index (GGGI). In 2017, under the patronage of the vice president, the UAE Gender Balance Council was launched to enhance the nation's efforts to drive women's participation in the development of the UAE, with the ultimate aim of having the UAE become one of the world's top 25 countries for gender equality by 2021 (UAE Cabinet, 2019).
 2 Al Oraimi (2011, p. 80).
 3 Schedneck (2013).
 4 Duffy (2012a).
 5 Brennen (2017, p. 161).
 6 Zelizer (2004).
 7 Ibid., p. 65.
 8 Leavy and Hesse-Biber (2011).
 9 Brennen (2017, p. 173).
10 A local term for an improper scheme or a policy-breaking expedient to gain an advantage.
11 A large glass-panelled office full of screens and technical equipment inside each newsroom is staffed by a team of editors, technicians, producers, and directors.
12 A local term for 'domestic news'.
13 Dubai One was created as a substitute for Dubai's Channel 33, which was launched in 1994 for the English-speaking audience. It broadcasts popular series and movies, as well as local news programmes.
14 These observations were documented solely with field notes.
15 Brennen (2017, p. 28).
16 BuMetea (2013, p. 14).
17 Founded in 2008 by the then-Abu Dhabi Media Company (now known as Abu Dhabi Media Network), in 2017, the UK's International Media Investments privatised it.
18 Founded in 1978 by Dubai's Al Nisr Publishing LLC.
19 For the full list of questions, see the appendix.
20 These testimonies are discussed at length in Chapters 5 and 6.
21 All interviews were conducted in Arabic, except for one. The quotes included in Chapters 5–8 were translated into English by the author.
22 Bottero (2005, p. 3).
23 For the full list of ages, see the appendix.

References

Al Oraimi, S. (2011). 'The Concept of Gender in Emirati Culture: An Analytical Study of the Role of the State in Redefining Gender and Social Roles'. *Museum International*, 63(3–4), pp. 78–92.

Bottero, W. (2005). *Stratification: Social Division and Inequality.* New York, NY: Routledge.

Brennen, B. (2017). *Qualitative Research Methods for Media Studies.* New York, NY: Routledge.

BuMetea, A. (2013). *Political Communication in the Arabian Gulf Countries.* Bloomington, IN: Xlibris LLC.

Duffy, M. (2012a). 'I've Been Kicked Out of the United Arab Emirates'. *Thoughts on Journalism, Culture and Global Communications.* 28 August. Available at: http://mattjduffy.com/2012/08/ive-been-kicked-out-of-the-united-arab-emirates/ [Accessed 19 September 2017].

Hassan, A. (2011). *Our Media Identity.* Dubai, UAE: Fujairah Media and Culture Authority.

Leavy, P. and Hesse-Biber, S. (2011). *The Practice of Qualitative Research*, 2nd edn. Thousand Oaks, CA: Sage.

Rugh, W. (2004). *Arab Mass Media: Newspapers, Radio, and Television in Arab Politics.* Westport, Conn, USA: Praeger.

Schedneck, J. (2013). 'Gender and Invested Agency: Cultural Expressions in the United Arab Emirates'. November. *Digital Library University of Adelaide.* Available at: https://digital.library.adelaide.edu.au/dspace/bitstream/2440/84319/9/01front.pdf [Accessed 4 January 2017].

UAE Cabinet. (2019). *Mohammed Bin Rashid Assigns the UAE Gender Balance Council to Oversee the Implementation of the 'Gender Inequality Index'.* UAE Cabinet Official Website. Available at: https://www.uaecabinet.ae/en/details/news/mohammed-bin-rashid-assigns-the-uae-gender-balance-council-to-oversee-the-implementation-of-the-gender-inequality-index [Accessed 23 December 2019].

Zelizer, B. (2004). *Taking Journalism Seriously.* Thousand Oaks, CA: Sage.

4   The Media Landscape and State Control

Despite the rapid development in its infrastructure from the 1970s onwards, the media environment in the Emirates has been seen as oppressive and unrepresentative due to the government's control over publications, leading the majority of journalists, men and women, locals and expats alike, to practice self-censorship in response to the intimidation they feel due to the laws and regulations that govern and restrict every media platform in the Emirates.

The Publication and Publishing Law issued by the Ministry of Information and Culture in November 1980 includes multiple articles which remain in effect that forbid challenging the supremacy of the state and its leaders. For instance, articles 70 and 71 declare: 'no criticism shall be made against the head of state or rulers of the Emirates', and 'any work is absolutely prohibited from being published if it involves instigation against Islam or the system of ruling, or if it causes harm to the interest of the state or the values of society'.[1] As for the nation's political affairs, according to articles 76 and 77:

> No article blemishing the president of an Arab, Islamic or any other friendly state will be published. It is also prohibited to publish any material that causes agitation to relations between the UAE and other Arab, Islamic and friendly countries. No article defaming Arabs and their civilization and heritage shall be published.[2]

Consequently, journalists consider self-censorship a normal practice, and the leading media outlets frequently publish government statements without criticism or comment. In a January 1980 column for *Al Azminah Al Arabiya* weekly magazine, Emirati journalist Mohammed Obaid Ghubash wrote:

> There is always the issue of sensitivity, or of topics being far too sensitive to be discussed, or written, and even published. So, eventually, journalists cannot practise their profession nor express their point of view freely, and end up writing reports using totally different languages and approaches aimed directly at executives and officials; and that is praise and glorification.[3]

DOI: 10.4324/9781003488415-4

In its relationship with the Emirati media, the state exercises political and financial power, in particular by directing top media corporations' officials, in both the Arabic and English-language press, about what type of content to publish and how it should be produced. In his study *The Relationship Between the Press and Political Authority in the UAE*, Emirati scholar A. Rashed describes how the government, on the one hand, obliges newspapers to publish the ministries' news with regard to their achievements, while, on the other hand, it prevents them from publishing any negative news dealing with national and regional security, such as border disputes and foreign military presence.[4]

Since the 1990s, rapid technological advances, the introduction of satellite television, and the growth of globalisation have made the state conscious of the importance of privatising the media in the Emirates to enhance its performance, reduce corporate bureaucracy, and make reporting more independent. To achieve these goals, free-media zones were launched in Abu Dhabi and Dubai, followed by the establishment of a media zone authority in 2007 meant to facilitate the growth of a diverse media industry in the Emirates. Meanwhile, state ministers have vocally championed media privatisation. Former Minister of Information Sheikh Abdullah bin Zayed Al Nahyan stated in 2001 that 'in the age of satellite television, governments can no longer control the dissemination of information to their citizens'. He contended that the public would 'no longer accept media that are seen as being government-controlled and which seek to provide them with a limited and partial view of events'.[5]

Still, achieving a free media environment, whether state-controlled or privatised, remains challenging due to the Emirates' authoritarian regime. The media industry bends to the influence of government financing as well as the strategic and political interests of owners and executives of media corporations such as Dubai Media City. As a result, freedom of expression is limited—media content is dominated by political news that serves the interests of the state, and the production of news is systematically constrained by restrictive newsroom routines and practices, including self-censorship.

The history of government control over the media

To elucidate the prevailing media environment from both historical and legal perspectives, this section assesses the evolution of the UAE press through three stages. The first stage, *the press and rulers*, reflects the direct involvement of Emirati rulers in developing the local press in the early years of nation-building through the allocation of generous printing budgets and the appointment of Emirati journalists to communicate the rulers' outlook on internal and external political matters. Examples include the ruler of Sharjah, Sheikh Sultan bin Mohammed Al Qassimi, who approved the publication of *Al Khaleej* newspaper in 1970 and appointed Emirati journalist Taryam Omran to mirror his strong political beliefs about Arab nationalism, the Palestinian cause, and the ideology of Nasserism.[6]

In the second stage, *the press and colonization*, the editorial content's primary focus was critiquing the British colonisation of the Trucial States and neighbouring Arab Gulf States, shedding light on issues like the political cupidity of the Iranians, who were clinging to the historical fact that the Gulf was known as Persian rather than Arabian, and to the presence of Americans in the area after the discovery of oil. Before the Emirates' political independence in 1971, newspaper articles alerted the local community about fabricated news that foreign powers like Britain and Iran aired via wireless radio stations in London, Tehran, and Ahvaz to distort the image of Arab nationalism and the revolts it inspired. A number of regional Arabic newspapers were banned from distribution, such as Egypt's *Al Joumhouria*, after it published an item by columnist Mamdouh Riza in January 1965 that questioned Iran's political avarice in the Arab Gulf states.[7]

The third and final stage, *the press and oil*, reflects the commercial association between the two. The discovery of oil and the consequent immense growth of public wealth created opportunities for newly established local entities and foreign businesses, such as oil companies and car showrooms, to reap quick profits. As a result, advertising in local newspapers, which had developed high-quality in-house printing facilities, boomed. The surge in demand for newspaper advertising space soon prompted most of the local newspapers to launch dedicated supplements specialising in business and economic news, boosting state revenues from advertising and driving greater regional distribution of Emirati newspapers throughout the 1980s and 1990s.[8]

With sweeping changes in the political environment across the Arab region since the millennium, Emirati journalists requested authorities amend the outdated 1980 media law. The requests were rejected, but on 25 September 2007, a sudden shift occurred, and a call for a new article within the current media law to prohibit the jailing of journalists was made by Sheikh Mohammed bin Rashid Al Maktoum, the Emirati Vice President, Prime Minister, and ruler of Dubai. Maktoum acted after two journalists working for Dubai's *Khaleej Times*, an English-language daily newspaper, were imprisoned for two months for libelling an Iranian woman. However, the vice president's call has not yet been made official as an Emiri (royal) decree, and thus the law has not been amended, leaving Emirati and expat journalists unprotected.[9]

After the rise of the Muslim Brotherhood to political power in Egypt in the aftermath of the 2010 Arab Spring, Reporters Without Borders declared that a number of journalists in the UAE had been arrested and jailed, while others had their passports confiscated and visas terminated. The authorities claimed that the journalists were imprisoned for supporting the Muslim Brotherhood, designated as a terrorist organisation by the Emirates. But to media observers, the Emirati authorities had persecuted journalists whose opinions were not in line with the authoritarian regime's political agenda, using the Anti-Terrorism Act of 2004 to limit freedom of expression.[10]

As a result, Emirati and expat journalists alike feel restricted in practising journalism in the Emirates, which was rated as 'not free'[11] by the US democracy advocacy group Freedom House in 2011 and ranked 112th out of 176 countries by the Paris-headquartered Reporters Without Borders. Due to the oppressive media environment, journalists do not act as watchdogs, the role assumed for them in the West—such a role is simply not recognised in the Emirates, just as it is not in the Arab Gulf states and Arab region more broadly. In a *Gulf News* column from 2010, Abdulkhaleq Abdulla wrote:

> Journalists are no longer doing their duty, meaning that the press is no longer monitoring the performance of the government. The government used its regulatory powers to cower the press and has done everything possible to gently court the media, keep it happy but under its tight benevolent watch. The government has made sure that the media does not develop an independent mind of its own.[12]

Given the absence of investigative journalism and reporters' intimidation by red lines and fear of deportation or imprisonment, censorship is effectively imposed over all types of information. This is reflected in journalists' day-to-day working methods. For instance, journalists often put a news story on hold and wait for it to be approved and released in advance by the official news agency of the Emirates, known by its Arabic abbreviation, WAM. If a news story is labelled as sensitive and thus disregarded by WAM, journalists follow their lead and avoid publishing it. These practices reflect the censorship system that the Emirati authorities have imposed on journalists and media corporations, leaving no need for a media police force to monitor them in-house, day and night.[13]

The findings on news production in the Emirates (discussed at length in the next four chapters) reflect national cultural values, as examined by Johan Galtung and Mari Holmboe Ruge in their 1965 study *The Structure of Foreign News*. Galtung and Ruge argued that there are cultural elements to the way that events are transmitted as news, stating that 'the more [an] event concerns elite people, the more probable that it will become a news item'.[14] The elite in this case are the ruling families and members of the cabinet elected by the Supreme Court, which comprises the rulers of the seven federal emirates. They set the local media agenda, provide the local media outlets with news in the form of events or statements, and play the role of sources for the local media outlets.

As a consequence, the concentration of political power in the Emirates after the federal union in 1971 has impacted news production and public opinion, as those in power benefit from the advanced media infrastructure to reinforce messages of patriotism and nationalism. There is a profound nationalist bias in Emirati news production, and Emirati journalists frequently put patriotism before professionalism. Loyalist news production reflects the ideological and cultural realities of Emiratis, who are labelled a minority in their own homeland due to the robust presence of Arab and foreign expats and the impact of globalisation on their national identity.[15]

With all these historical changes, why were Emirati women specifically off the pace in contributing to the press? I argue that Emirati women were very late in endorsing the concepts of intellectual liberty and equality that Arab feminists like Hind Nawfal, Huda Shaarawi, Faiza Nabrawi, Doria Shafiq, and Ghanima Al

Marzouk championed in the early to mid-twentieth century, due to the lack of educational opportunities and the persistence of patriarchy in the Emirates.

Before the discovery of oil, Emirati women participated in collective economic duties in addition to their traditional domestic roles because difficult economic conditions forced many Emirati men to travel for months for pearl diving expeditions or trading. Taking up these roles did not mean that Emirati women became decision-makers, but rather social negotiators who practised these duties solely by virtue of the financial demands of the time, not concepts of equality or women's rights. After the discovery of oil, Emirati women's participation in collective duties decreased, and they again became more financially dependent on men. The dramatic shift in the economy reaffirmed the tribal patriarchal system.[16]

Censored media cultures have an especially stifling effect on Emirati women's contribution to the arts and literature, the practice and production of which remains rare amongst Emirati women today, as it was decades ago before the country's independence in 1971. Due to tribal and traditional restrictions, Emirati women lived in isolated, segregated circumstances, which made it difficult for them to publish literary works unless under pseudonyms to avoid social prejudice. Moreover, the historically high rate of illiteracy limited Emirati women's creativity. Access to homeschooling, before the establishment of government-funded schools, was available only to Emirati women who belonged to families privileged by either their alliance with the royal family through politically arranged marriages or their prosperous businesses and inherited wealth. And even these privileged Emirati women were reluctant to publish their work—mainly poetry—under their real names.

Nevertheless, the local cultural scene witnessed the emergence of two waves of creative Emirati women writers between the 1960s and the late 1980s, viewed as the golden age of literature and the journalism movement in the Emirates. Leading figures included poet Ousha bint Khalifa Al Suwaidi, who published a series of Nabatean[17] poems in the early 1970s under the nickname Bint Al Arab (daughter of Arabs), and novelists Amaal Khalid Al Qassimi and Nama Al Qassimi.[18]

Furthermore, the launch of the Emirates Writers Union in 1984 with 30 active members[19] seemed to herald greater freedoms for the second wave of creative Emirati writers, men and women alike. However, literary production and investigative journalism remained rare because of censorship and the fear of punishment under the media law. In 1973, for instance, a group of young Emirati journalists led by Dr. Mohamed Obaid Ghubash had launched *Al Majmaa* (Assembly), a weekly magazine that published numerous political and cultural features with a sharp, critical tone that surprised the local community. It was closed after two years by the Ministry of Culture and Information (which was replaced in 2006 by the National Media Council (NMC).

Al Azminah Al Arabiya was another politically focused weekly magazine that endorsed the writing talents of Emirati female journalists, including Khairiyah Rabei from the northern emirate of Ajman, who wrote major stories about Palestinian women's rights, as well as Dr. Rafia Obaid Ghubash, Dr. Hessa Abdullah Lootah, and Hala Humaid, who wrote items that focused on art and literature. The magazine was banned from publishing in October 1981 after featuring a cover story celebrating the assassination of Egypt's President Muhammad Anwar El Sadat. While Sadat had been widely portrayed in the Arab press as a betrayer of Arab unity since signing a peace treaty with Israel at Camp David in 1979, *Al Azminah Al Arabiya*'s story—with its bold headline, 'The Arabs' Betrayer Has Fallen'[20]—evidently crossed a line.

Emirati journalists are effectively barred from pursuing investigative journalism in a field that is shadowed by tribal political loyalty and censorship, reflected in the fact that the UAE Journalists Association (UAEJA) had 58 active members at its late inauguration in January 2000,[21] a number that had increased to only 372 by 2018.[22]

The code of ethics and journalism practices

News production in the Emirates is systematic—whether broadcast in Arabic or English, the format of producing and publishing news is standardised and in line with the authoritarian state's political and socio-cultural agendas. Media content is monitored and controlled through a series of government channels, such as the NMC, which sets press regulations; the Emirates News Agency (WAM), the country's official news agency; and the Security Media Department, which is operated by the Ministry of Interior.

Attempts to publish independent and investigative news have faced major obstacles, as in the case of Dubai's free English-language tabloid *7 Days*, launched in 2004 by the UK's General Trust and the *Daily Mail*. When the daily published news features concerning workers' abuse and prostitution in Dubai, it was suspended temporarily, and managing editors practised self-censorship to avoid provoking the authorities further.[23] After 14 years of operation, on 22 December 2016, the paper shut down.

As a result, the process of news production is almost entirely orchestrated by those in political power, and the practice of journalism is distorted due to corporate policies designed to please the state and the narrow scope of 'legitimate' news sources, who invariably reflect the interests of the authoritarian regime. This media reality has become the norm inside Emirati newsrooms and is evident in the articles of the Charter of Honour and Code of Ethics,[24] released by the UAEJA in 2008. As explained in Chapter 2, journalists and press agencies in the Emirates have complied for decades with the 1980 Printing Press and Publication Law, according to which the Ministry of Information and Culture controls the ownership of media outlets through strict licencing provisions.

Not only is the ownership of media outlets controlled, but the ministry also demands that the identity of journalists be revealed and the publication of press materials be monitored at all times by its censors, who, according to the law, 'are empowered to confiscate materials and tools used in committing offences'.[25] Article 9 of the law states that 'the owner of the printing press shall keep a record stamped by the ministry, to record titles of material pending publishing, names of the material originators and number of copies printed from that material. The owner shall submit the record to the proper authority at the ministry'.[26] And Article 11 states that 'ten copies of the published material shall be submitted by the printing house to the censorship department at the ministry',[27] facilitating censors' decision-making.

In Chapters 4 and 7 of the 1980 law, a set of articles, while not clearly identified as a journalistic code of ethics, are generally understood that way, and the Emirati and expat journalists observed and interviewed for this study adhered to them as such, as the following chapters describe. For example, Article 28 states that a journalist shall not commit 'an offence involving moral turpitude' for which he or she is liable to be 'ordered to leave the country for an offence related to publishing'.[28] Articles 72 and 73 state that 'no opinions shall be published if they violate public discipline and order, or involve insult, or call for or circulate subversive ideas', or incite 'dissension among individuals of society'.[29]

In addition, journalists in the Emirates are required to be impartial while reporting so as not to 'publish in bad faith any false news, or forge or tamper documents' or 'cause damage to the national economy',[30] as stated in articles 80 and 81 of the 1980 law. Articles 82 and 84 dictate that journalists should not use in writing 'any phrases, expressions or pictures that are inconsistent with public conduct, or mislead the public',[31] or write news to criticise 'a public official, or anybody occupying a post in the public prosecution'.[32] Failing to comply with the law may result in the imprisonment of the journalist and editor-in-chief, the imposition of severe fines, and the closure of the offending newspaper.[33]

The 1980 law states that the media is 'free'—'within the limits' of the law itself.[34] Any media organ, however, is subject to grave punishment if it

> defames Islamic beliefs or incites hatred against the system of ruling, or causes harm to the supreme interests of the country, or publishes materials that cause damage to the constitution, particularly to the concept of unity and federation, or threatens public order, or serves foreign interests that contradict national interests, or publishes ideas of a hostile country, or discloses military secrets, or publishes materials that cause confusion among the public.[35]

The release of the 26 articles of the Charter of Honour and Code of Ethics in 2008, as mentioned, did not unshackle the media. Rather, the code demands that journalists practise their profession responsibly and in line with the government's policies to sustain social stability and resist any perceived threats. For instance, Article 10 states that 'journalists should not seek to provoke or inflame public feelings by any means. They should not use the media for the purpose of libel or slandering'.[36] Similarly, Article 12 declares that 'journalists should be very vigilant to traps of discrimination and avoid involving themselves by any means in any stories hinting at discrimination of race, sex, language, faith or national and social background'.[37]

The 2008 Code of Ethics also emphasises the role of responsible reporting from a professional perspective, but it failed to take the opportunity to widen the limited scope for practising investigative journalism or exercising freedom of expression.

Rather, it appears to encourage self-censorship and afford little protection of rights. Though Article 2 asserts that 'the journalist must commit himself at all times to the principles of *freedom* in gathering and publishing stories',[38] the meaning of 'freedom' here is left entirely vague.

Article 23, meanwhile, cautions that a 'journalist has to do his best not to become part of a story, and to cover news not make it'.[39] This would seem to bar the journalist from serving as society's watchdog for justice and ensure that media content across every platform, including social media, is uncritical. This is underscored by Article 4, which asserts that a journalist 'should only use legitimate means to obtain information, photos and documents from original sources'.[40] This means that items released and approved by the authorities are the journalist's only legitimate sources for politically significant news reports.

The remaining codes explain the professional values for journalists in the Emirates and what qualifies as journalistic integrity. In abiding by the Charter of Honour and Code of Ethics, journalists in the Emirates must notably agree to 'respect the privacy of individuals and not expose them by publishing anything without the consent of those individuals'.[41]

In addition, multiple articles in the charter regulate journalistic practices inside the newsroom and the publication of news in the Emirates on the basis of respect for its society and religion. Article 18 asserts that 'Islam is a basic and important component of UAE culture, values, and traditions, and respect of divine religions and traditions and values of nations takes centre stage as a mandatory code of ethics for the media and should not be offended or desecrated in any form'.[42]

Particularly vexing issues related to journalistic competition arise in cases where expat journalists, Arabs included, practise a form of shadowing with the aim of teaching journalism to Emirati journalists from their own perspective, bringing to the fore the differences in their prior journalistic experiences. These might have involved working in fear under a dictatorship that forced them to practise self-censorship. Alternatively, they might have been in a democratic nation that allowed them to play key roles as watchdogs and change-makers, working to bring about political and socio-cultural progress within their society.

This has created further issues inside the newsroom amongst Emirati and expat journalists, where professional competition in producing significant and hard-edged news stories is coloured by ethnic and national stereotypes. For instance, Arab journalists from the Levant are believed to be far more proficient in gathering and analysing news in the Arabic language, whether in print or in broadcast media. The intensity of their presence in the newsroom and at local media corporations has created an aura of monopoly that leaves Emirati journalists feeling underrepresented and discriminated against in terms of career development. Some are confused, as well, as they try to figure out their national identity while being challenged to balance the preservation of their ancient heritage and traditions in the present-day context of multiculturalism and diversity (see Chapter 5).

The challenge of professional stereotyping extends to local newsrooms, where media content is produced in English. Emirati journalists, young graduates, in particular, feel underrepresented, despite their competence in producing and writing news stories for English-run television channels and dailies. This is due to the ubiquity of expats in managing the editorial newsrooms. In addition, many expats in English-speaking newsrooms comply with criticism-free journalism to toe the line of the government's policies. They often avoid discussion of topics that are considered religiously and culturally sensitive to protect themselves from deportation or imprisonment. Young Emirati media graduates' chances to engage in investigative journalism are thus limited even at privately owned, non-Arabic newspapers, compounding the confusion they must experience after spending years in school studying media ethics and free speech.

In sum, the content of the bilingual print media, daily newspapers in particular, and local news broadcasting in the Emirates is a loyalist to a fault. The safest sort of domestic stories dominate, such as those concerning ministerial activities and announcements by the royal court and federal authorities, alongside coverage of events of social interest including health, employment, education, sports, and culture. Some daily newspapers dedicate a few pages to cover international news of concern to the expat communities, such as events in India, Pakistan, or the Philippines.

The emergence of social media platforms has altered the coverage of local news as residents, Emiratis, and expats alike post photos and videos of current events in an attempt to sway public opinion and provoke decision-makers such as the members of the parliament at the Federal National Council. They are assisting traditional journalists by eluding some of the limitations on news coverage of often neglected issues such as migrant workers' rights and the Emiratising of vital economic sectors.

The authorities' intense media surveillance, including that of social media platforms such as X (formerly Twitter), has added to the list of challenges faced by those who value press freedom and best journalistic practices. While most Emirati journalists practise self-censorship assiduously, a number of Emirati social media activists have been detained or imprisoned for spreading false news and cyber-crime-related violations—for example, Obaid Al Zaabi, who criticised the lack of free speech in the Emirates during a CNN interview in 2013.[43] Several international journalists who have tackled unpleasant issues in the Emirates have been deported as a result, amongst them Irish journalist Sean O'Driscoll, whose investigative feature about the inhumane treatment of migrant labourers in Abu Dhabi was published by *The Guardian* in 2014.[44]

Conclusion

Defining the roles and responsibilities of journalists in the Emirates remains contestable. The government and political elite's influence over the media environment through subsidies and censorship exacerbates the situation, as the state aims to protect the public from what it sees as external socio-political threats transmitted by the regional and international media.

Understandably, the state fears that these forces can undermine Emirati society's unity and sense of identity. At the same time, the state wants to turn the Emirates into a media hub that hosts internationally respected channels and news agencies such as CNN, BBC, and Reuters and to expand the art, entertainment, and cultural scenes in the country, in turn spurring growth in tourism and other non-oil sectors.

Through the control of the media, the state can create a tailored media context that serves its propaganda aims. Since 2019, for instance, 'tolerance'—particularly in regard to religious diversity and freedom—has been used heavily as a brand by the government. Through this brand, the state has positioned itself as an international political power player, embracing all faiths, including Judaism, and launching projects such as the Abrahamic Family House, where a mosque, church, and synagogue have been built in one place for the first time in the Gulf region. The three sacred spaces—Imam Al Tayeb Mosque, St. Francis Church, and Moses ben Maimon Synagogue—were officially inaugurated on 16 February 2023,[45] a significant development prompted by the 2020 signing of the Abraham Accord between the UAE and Israel.

Notes

1 UAE Federal Government (1980, p. 19). All translations of the media law by the author.
2 Ezzat (1983, pp. 131–132). Translated by the author.
3 BuMetea (2013, p. 25).
4 BuMetea (2013, p. 25).
5 Rugh (2004, p. 65).
6 Ezzat (1983).
7 Ibid.
8 Ibid.
9 Puddington et al. (2008, p. 340).
10 Gasiorowski (2017, p. 367).
11 Duffy (2014, p. 29).
12 Ibid., p. 53.
13 Ibid.
14 Clausen (2003, p. 46).
15 Gulf News (2008).
16 Al Oraimi (2011).
17 Poetry written in Emirati dialect.
18 Salih (1983).
19 Gulf News (2012).
20 Salih (1983, p. 375).
21 UAE Journalists Association (2019).
22 Abdelhamid (2018).
23 Oxford Business Group (2007, p. 211).
24 The UAE's Charter of Honour and Code of Ethics for the media differs from the Code of Ethics and Professional Conduct, which was issued by the Federal Authority for Government Human Resources in 2010 for civil services in the UAE.
25 UAE Federal Government (1980, p. 17).
26 Ibid., p. 3.
27 Ibid., p. 4.
28 Ibid., p. 18.
29 Ibid.
30 Ibid., p. 19.
31 Ibid.
32 Ibid., p. 20.
33 Ibid., p. 2.
34 Ibid., p. 25.
35 Ibid., p. 23.

36 Gulf News (2008).
37 Ibid.
38 Ibid.
39 Ibid.
40 Ibid.
41 Ibid.
42 Ibid.
43 Duffy (2014).
44 Schlanger (2015).
45 Sankar and Maxwell (2023).

References

Abdelhamid, M. (2018). 'Election of a New Board for the Journalists' Association'. *Al Bayan*, 2 March. Translated by the author. Available at: https://www.albayan.ae/across-the-uae/news-and-reports/2018-03-02-1.3199683 [Accessed 17 February 2019].

Al Oraimi, S. (2011). 'The Concept of Gender in Emirati Culture: An Analytical Study of the Role of the State in Redefining Gender and Social Roles'. *Museum International*, 63(3–4).

BuMetea, A. (2013). *Political Communication in the Arabian Gulf Countries*. Bloomington, IN: Xlibris LLC.

Clausen, L. (2003). *Global News Production*. Copenhagen: Copenhagen Business School Press.

Duffy, M. (2014). *Media Law in the United Arab Emirates*. Alphen aan den Rijn, the Netherlands: Kluwer Law International.

Ezzat, A. (1983). *Journalism in the Arab Gulf States. Translated by the author*. Baghdad: Gulf States Information Documentation Centre.

Gasiorowski, M. (2017). *The Government and Politics of the Middle East and North Africa*. Boulder, CO: Westview Press.

Gulf News (2008). *Code of Ethics*. 20 January. Available at: https://gulfnews.com/uae/code-of-ethics-1.78730 [Accessed 5 July 2020].

Gulf News (2012). *The UAE Writers Union*. 27 December. Available at: https://gulfnews.com/uae/the-uae-writers-union-1.1124627 [Accessed 15 February 2019].

Oxford Business Group (2007). *The Report: Dubai 2007*. London.

Puddington, A., Piano, A., Eiss, C., Neubauer, K. and Roylance, T. (2008). *Freedom in the World 2008*. New York, NY: Freedom House.

Salih, L. (1983). *Women's Literature in the Arab Gulf.* Translated by the author. Kuwait City: Dar Al Yaqatha Publications.

Sankar, A. and Maxwell, C. (2023) 'UAE's Abrahamic Family House Opens to the Public', *The National*. Available at: https://www.thenationalnews.com/uae/2023/02/17/uaes-abrahamic-family-house-to-open-on-march-1 [Accessed: 3 February 2024].

Schlanger, Z. (2015). 'Under Surveillance in Abu Dhabi: A Reporter's Saga of Being Followed, Bribed, and Recruited as a Spy'. *Newsweek*. 30 March. Available at: https://www.newsweek.com/under-surveillance-abu-dhabi-reporters-saga-being-followed-bribed-and-317627 [Accessed 20 July 2020].

UAE Federal Government (1980). *Federal Law No. 15 For 1980 Concerning Publications and Publishing*. Abu Dhabi: Ministry of Information and Culture.

UAE Journalists Association (2019). *About Us*. Translated by the author. UAE Journalists Association Official Website. Available at: https://uaeja.org/ar/pages/6/ [Accessed 17 February 2019].

5   The Ultimate Question

Who's in Charge?

Throughout history and up to this day, female journalists have shared similar experiences: being exposed to patriarchal gender bias inside the newsroom and treated as inferiors because of their gender, their empathy, their sensitivity, and their communication skills. Despite the crucial work of trailblazing investigative journalists such as Kuwait's Nouria Al Saddani and the UK's Kate Ironside and those who have followed to provide the public with news that reflects both positive and negative societal realities, female journalists encounter continuing resistance from misogynists who occupy leading positions in media corporations, who practise intentional institutionalised engagements inside the newsroom, and who have disempowered them at every opportunity, simply because their journalistic talents are seen as a threat.

Female journalists' experiences register the mindset of misogyny and sexism they confront, a universal phenomenon in which men fear the rise of women and impose limits on their capabilities. Men assign women the role of exclusively sexual, seductive beings, insisting that women's nature requires them to master the art of what is cast as genetic inferiority by silencing their own voices and acting powerless. Since at least as far back as the evolution of monotheism, lawmakers and theologians have disseminated the concept of men's superiority to facilitate women's oppression.

The gendered elements of newsroom practices such as gender stereotyping and clustering, sexism, and misogyny lead female journalists to act as social passivists, tolerating not only psychological restrictions that make them feel embarrassed, humiliated, and pressured[1] but also institutional engagements in the workplace that limit decision-making and expose them to condescension and disrespect. Saudi female journalist Manal Al Sharif, who worked for *Al Watan* newspaper between 2005 and 2017, shed light on the widely shared experience of institutionalised engagements that encourage social passivity on the part of female journalists everywhere. Al Sharif criticised the Saudi government for neglecting to investigate the condition of female journalists in Saudi media corporations, where they are disrespected professionally and their rights for equal pay are dismissed.

A 2012 study found that women comprised only 22 percent of the voices heard and read in the news around the Arab world.[2] The field observations and

DOI: 10.4324/9781003488415-5

in-depth interviews with Emirati and Arab expat female journalists conducted for this study demonstrate that women remain sorely underrepresented and held back in the media. They are eclipsed in hard news and portrayed in the most superficial ways in the 'women's media' that targets them. In the latter, women's presence is limited to gendered news coverage of topics like childcare, family welfare, fashion, and cookery. Alternatively, they are portrayed as beauty objects, especially those who work as news anchors and broadcasters for talk shows dedicated mainly to women. The struggle for equal representation inside the newsroom, on the one hand, and the accurate portrayal of women in the media, on the other, are universal.

Beauty over brains

The media plays an influential role in maintaining gendered conceptions and stereotypes, not only about professional roles but also about appearance, promoting for women an unrealistic, flawless, and ultimately sexist image on television through the discriminating selection of newsreaders.[3] This is evident on Arab news broadcasting channels, where 'female presenters have become the dream girls or model women for Arab teenagers and young men in general, who view Arab female presenters as the model of beauty they seek in their dream girl'.[4] Al Jazeera newsreader Khadijah bin Guenna has suggested that female presenters are used as 'eye candy for the viewers' by some satellite television networks, which 'give women jobs that require wearing a smile all the time, or on the basis of external beauty'.[5]

The importance that Arab satellite television networks place on female beauty was demonstrated by the decision of the Egyptian Radio and Television Union (ERTU) to suspend eight female television presenters who had been attacked on social media and labelled *bakabozza*, Egyptian slang for 'fat' or 'overweight'. To protect the reputation of Egyptian state television, the presenters, who included Mervat Negm and Yomna Hassan from Channel One and Khadija Khattab and Sara El Hilali from Channel Two, were ordered to follow a weight loss plan for a month and resume work only once they had achieved the standards of appearance set by the broadcaster.[6]

The portrayal of female news anchors and broadcasters as eye candy or dream girls was apparent when I observed Emirati female news anchors' heavy eye makeup and embroidered veils at the Abu Dhabi and Dubai news centres. They seem to accept their treatment as beauty objects and do not find it discriminatory, emphasising their glamour as opposed to their intellectual power. The Emirati female news anchors I observed are evidently concerned with their makeup, hair, and clothing. They tend not to follow the professional dress and makeup codes given to them by what is known as the 'appearance department' at both news centres, preferring to outsource to local designers for their attire, often a popular designer boutique, which will receive credit at the end of the local news broadcast. In addition, they don't depend on the makeup professionals employed by the studios, preferring popular Lebanese or Emirati makeup artists who specialise in weddings and special events.

This focus on costumes and cosmetics has itself become a source of laughter and teasing amongst male colleagues. In the Abu Dhabi newsroom, a senior male editor joked, as an Emirati female news anchor was busy adjusting her makeup, that she need not bother. Then, in front of the entire team in the newsroom, he peeked into her small Harrods utility bag, took her perfume, and tried it on himself. Certainly, Emirati male news anchors also pay attention to their appearance. On one occasion, during a commercial break, I observed a young anchor for Dubai's *Akhbar Al Emarat* looking in a mirror hidden under the table to adjust his traditional headdress, known in the region as a *ghutra*,[7] and then start taking selfies for his followers on Instagram. The management at both news centres consistently chooses as anchors young, attractive Emirati men and women who conform to the ideal body shape, perpetuating the valuation—and stereotype—of beauty over brains.

Observing Emirati male and female news anchors' attitudes towards working in the newsroom raises the question of why women's beauty, specifically, is prized in the broadcast media in a religious, conservative culture. Considering the issue in 2014, Emirati writer and media critic Maryam Al Kaabi argued that 'the Arab media is filled with fakes where beauty is given priority over substance, compromising the seriousness of the contents', and that 'capitalism had led Arab satellite television networks to use women as attractive commodities to increase audience ratings'.[8]

The bullying and undermining of female journalists' intellectual strengths by focusing on their biological nature and feminine attributes took place inside the newsrooms of local media corporations, where several Emirati and Arab expat female journalists affirmed having experienced direct verbal harassment that belittled their creative work and discrimination and misogyny that barred them from promotional opportunities. At the same time, external male sources resisted communicating with female journalists, apparently viewing them as unreliable and incompetent in reporting political and economic news.

At the beginning of her career in 2002, Rawdha, who chose to use a pseudonym for the study, experienced verbal harassment by Emirati and Arab expat male colleagues, as well as male sources, when she worked as a journalist for a leading Emirati newspaper, covering both entertainment and the economy. She described how, when she managed to secure a rare exclusive interview with a major Arab politician, 'the entire editorial content with quotations was never published in the newspaper! I knew later that an Emirati male senior editor did not want my name and profile as a journalist to be raised'.

Because of a lack of credit she endured inside the newsroom, Rawdha decided to return to her newspaper's entertainment section, where she began her journalistic career. Her productivity declined, and she was exposed to another form of abuse and bullying: visual sexual harassment by male journalists who made inappropriate remarks about her physical appearance. Rawdha felt unsafe and uncomfortable reporting it. She remembered:

When I ate my lunch, for instance, a male colleague would tell me, 'You have gained weight!', or would stare at me in a curious way and ask me: 'Are your eyelashes real or fake?' … There was another male colleague [who] specialized in writing poetry columns for the newspaper's weekly culture supplement. To my embarrassment, he would often sign his poetry column with the words *Dedicated to* [her first initial], print the press clipping, and leave it on my desk.

Asserting that a woman was too beautiful to have brains was another form of bullying those male journalists would often use to demean their female colleagues' intellect and journalistic ability, as in the case of Yusra Adil, the editor of external politics at *Al Ittihad*. At the beginning of her career at the newspaper in 2011, Adil's editorial features on international politics were never published due to male jealousy, and she was offered a promotion only if she agreed to write for another section. 'They would say: "You are a girl! What do you want to do with politics!" One male colleague said to me: "You are very pretty, why don't you write in entertainment instead of politics?"'

Female journalists also often found it difficult to access the sources that provide information, exclusive interview opportunities, and press statements, negatively affecting the quality of their performance and rate of production. Rasha Tubeileh, a Jordanian journalist for *Al Ittihad*, faced this sort of challenge early in her career when she worked for *Alghad* newspaper in Amman. She described how sources refused to work with her solely because she was a young woman.

Female journalists' struggle to break through and be heard was evident in the Emirati broadcast media too, where the female voice is generally considered undesirable unless it is applied to a human-interest story. As reporter Mahra Al Jenaibi, who works for Abu Dhabi Television Channel One and has been reporting for the *Oloum Al Dar* news program since 2014, described: 'Observe the *Oloum Al Dar* news broadcast, and you will find that only male reporters appear in reports relating to the royal court and the rulers. Female reporters don't appear in such reports, not even to do the voice-overs'.

Gender disparity and institutionalised sexism

The gender politics faced by female journalists inside the newsroom, in sum, tended to render them marginal.[9] The daunting experiences of gender stereotyping, gender clustering, discrimination, and trivialisation were repeatedly described by the 30 women journalists who participated in the semi-structured interviews. For instance, Lahib Abdulkhaliq, an Iraqi editor of external politics for *Al Ittihad* newspaper, who has more than 30 years of experience in political journalism and written two books, *Between Two Collapses: The New American Strategy* and *The Blood Sociology,* explained that working for *Al Ittihad* became a nightmare because of one Arab expat male chief editor, who barred her from promotion simply for being a woman. She said:

I was downgraded from a grade five senior editor to a grade seven journalist. I used to get a pay check of 35,000 dirhams per month [about £7,000], and now I only get a pay check of 18,000 dirhams per month [about £3,000]. I've been suffering from this unfair treatment since 2008. The current [Arab expat] chief editor was a journalist with no experience whatsoever in politics or political analytics, and he was the one who manipulated the promotions list, as well as my job contract.

Senior *Al Ittihad* business journalist Reem Al Breiki strongly believes that the media industry in the Emirates is full of misogynists who simply think of women as incapable. However, she blames women for accepting the concept of shame, or *ayeb*, to the extent of denying themselves every opportunity to rise, while 'my male colleagues would avoid contacting me at night to discuss work-related issues, thinking that I had commitments at home with my husband and family'. Al Breiki was treated unfairly, demoted, and investigated by her former managers. She described what happened when her newspaper:

planned to expel a number of Emirati journalists from the older genera-tion, including myself, to bring in 'new blood'! I stood against this unfair treatment ... and I was demoted. Promotions were granted randomly, based on favouritism. I faced verbal harassment and rumours inside the newsroom which aimed to 'teach me a lesson'! Then I was suspended from work for three months, while an investigation took place. I was innocent of all the charges put against me; they created a case out of nothing, simply because I defended the older Emirati female journalists at the newspaper, who were treated unfairly. We wrote a grievance letter against the management, which was eventually replaced after all these events.

Leila, an executive news editor at the Emirates News Agency (WAM) with a degree from a British university who preferred to use a pseudonym to hide her real identity, described stepping down as acting head of an important bureau only six months after taking the position: 'It was a very big decision for me.... One of the reasons why I decided to step down was because I didn't feel I was being recognized or encouraged or given credit for my work.... There was a lot of re-sistance from the misogynistic older men that I managed, basically. They didn't like it, to have a female head'. Leila and the other UAE-based female journalists interviewed for this study extensively recounted their experiences with the glass ceiling that resulted in limiting their career progression, thwarting their access to the sorts of assignments that lead to greater stature and eventually promotions, a problem shared by many of their female counterparts elsewhere.

Female journalists worldwide are frequently blocked from leading positions at media corporations because of gendered stereotypes concerning their perfor-mance in the workplace. In particular, they are often regarded as incompetent due to being distracted by family commitments. This renders female journalists in the eyes of the executives unfit and unqualified; ultimately, they are often dismissed. In the Middle East and North Africa (MENA), the obstacles posed by the glass ceiling and constraints on women's accepted roles in media are severe. In the Emirates, media women, Emiratis, and Arab expats alike are often refused promotional opportunities despite having outstanding qualifications. It was only recently, in 2016, that Emirati journalist Muna Busamra became the first and only female editor-in-chief in the history of Dubai's *Al Bayan* newspaper and Emirati journalism at large. Moreover, out of the 30 Emirati and Arab expat female journalists that were interviewed for this book, only four currently hold leading positions: Fatema Al Senani, head of operations projects at Abu Dhabi Media Company (ADMC); Ameena Awadh Bin Amro, head of electronic publishing at *Al Ittihad* newspaper; Heyam Obaid Bawazir, head of news output at Abu Dhabi Television Channel One; and Hala Al Gergawi, executive managing editor and editor-in-chief of *Zahrat Al Khaleej* magazine.

Emirati and Arab expat female journalists are conscious of gender disparity, sexism, and misogyny in the newsroom, as practised by Emirati and Arab expat male journalists alike, directly and indirectly. However, they are anxious about reporting even unambiguous transgressions for various reasons, including social stigma (the shame, or *ayeb*), fear of job and income loss, and family and community pressures.

Prior to joining *Al Ittihad* as an editor of external politics, Lahib Abdulkhaliq worked at Dubai's *Al Bayan* newspaper from 1999 to 2005, where she became the first female journalist to head the reporters' section that reported on international political news, with 25 reporters under her supervision. At *Al Bayan*, she edited a four-page weekly political supplement known as 'The Wednesday Strategic', and succeeded in conducting an exclusive interview with Taha Yasin Ramadan,[10] the first interview with a high-ranking Iraqi official to be published in a Gulf state newspaper since the Second Gulf War. However, she felt suffocated upon taking up her new position at *Al Ittihad* because of the misogynistic treatment. She said:

> I faced a cruel battle here [*Al Ittihad*] because I became very popular, more than my male chief editor. There was and still is a level of jealousy. At one point, the former editor-in-chief asked my chief editor to assign me to write a three-page political feature, but he never told me about this particular assignment.... When I confronted the former editor-in-chief, he told me that my chief editor had made two different excuses: one, that I cannot write this political feature due to a lack of knowledge, and two, that I don't have the time to write it because of other deadlines.
>
> Because of him, I had constant disputes with the former editor-in-chief. They published all the political features that I wrote and analysed ... without my name. Some colleagues took my side in these disputes, and whenever the chief editor was absent on annual leave, they would print my name on the political features that I wrote, telling me: 'Write whatever you like, and we will ensure that your name is printed as long as he's away!' I feel trapped and the chief editor doesn't want me to become popular in fear of losing his position and chair!

Rasha Tubeileh observed:

> In terms of promotions, there is a level of discrimination. You will rarely find
> a woman in the position of editor-in-chief. Women's presence is increasing,
> but they do not take a vital role in leadership positions. [At *Al Ittihad*], the
> only female senior editor is Mouzah Matar,[11] who works at the newspaper's
> Dubai office. I think it is related to two factors: the strong competition be-
> tween men and women, and the social constraints like marriage and parent-
> hood that hold women back from thinking about their career ambitions.

Jalila, a Jordanian editor at *Al Ittihad* who received an award for her work in
hard news, has experienced her own share of male jealousy and institutionalised
sexism inside the newsroom. Gender politics at *Al Ittihad* have cost Jalila (a pseudonym) her job. She said:

> In this field, men treat me as incapable and unqualified because, simply, they
> think that I cannot do my job at night! On one occasion, for instance, I stayed
> late at work—until 8 p.m. A male colleague, an Egyptian, came across and
> said to me: 'Please leave the office. I cannot bear the thought of seeing you
> away from your daughters!' I replied: 'You don't have the right to think that
> you care about my daughters more than I do.' His intentions were not inno-
> cent, but malicious, aimed at the managing editor, to make him question the
> capabilities of female journalists. I was eventually downgraded from the post
> of supervisor, which was later given to a male colleague, simply because of
> these perceptions.
>
> You need to understand that these messages that male colleagues flash
> all over the office are not sympathetic, but aimed at the managing editors to
> use their powers to give out promotions, and to eventually get rid of female
> journalists because their husbands can support them financially. Because of
> these perceptions, I tried to change the feminine side of my personality; I
> wore unstylish and unflattering clothes, and wore no makeup at all, so that
> the focus would move away from my body.

A number of female journalists interviewed for this book had to put up with misogynistic bosses, including Rawdha, whose Emirati editor-in-chief was notorious
for his open opposition to women's empowerment. She remembered:

> The former editor-in-chief of *Al Ittihad* newspaper was a misogynist. He dis-
> liked the idea of empowering women, and never allowed female journalists
> to reach leading positions in the newspaper, especially as section heads. He
> believed that men deserved to take the lead because they are simply better at
> doing the job, especially late at night! I managed a supplement for four years,
> and my job title remained the same, a journalist. Instead of promoting me,
> the former editor-in-chief hired a male journalist from [outside the UAE] for
> the position, giving him the title of chief editor, just because he was a male.

But for Ameena Awadh Bin Amro, head of electronic publishing at *Al Ittihad*, the challenges that media women face have nothing to do with genderisation, male dominance, or living in a patriarchal society. To her, it is women's problem:

> The restrictions imposed on women journalists are not corporate or related to the law; on the contrary, there is no such inequality and our salaries are the same. However, the restrictions are self-imposed; they are not even imposed by the family or society. Women and men alike face self-imposed restrictions in accepting one another, I think. Women too put on such restrictions and link it to marriage or the superiority of the husbands. Women need to resist these self-imposed restrictions, first, in order to achieve empowerment. The promotional and economic rights are equal. I'm the only woman at *Al Ittihad* to hold the position of head of electronic publishing. To me, only the best professionals who follow best practises in their career have the right to claim a promotion.

K.T., a Moroccan law school graduate and senior journalist at *Al Ittihad*, has a different opinion—she feels that men often practise discrimination due to beliefs acquired as far back as childhood. She said:

> There is a level of discomfort with women due to men's mentality and perceptions. I mean some men were raised in patriarchal, male-dominated surroundings, and that in itself has influenced their character. They don't accept the concept of women's emancipation and are often jealous of women's success. I also witness such perceptions when tasks are distributed. Female journalists are not preferred to cover news stories abroad in Japan and the USA for instance. Male journalists are far more preferred for overseas jobs.
>
> We are not encouraged to write outstanding investigative features, which eventually kills the spirit of motivation in any journalist. On one occasion, I took the initiative to attend a two-day conference to cover a certain topic, but my chief editor was not pleased about my absence from the office, and told me to follow the work schedule that he created for me. The chief editor assumed that I attend conferences for tea and chitchats! That is the male mentality!

The opposite sex rethinks integration

Most of the male journalists who were interviewed for this book argued that certain roles are male-dominant inside the newsroom. This, they opined, was justified by social norms, which editors and executives must adhere to. Yousef Bustangi, an experienced Palestinian business reporter for *Al Ittihad*, whose career began in 1992, explained: 'Arab women maintain family commitments more than Arab men; that's why men get more space and chances to shine in the workplace, not because of gender inequality. Raising children, for instance, would restrict your chances to work out in the field, or to travel abroad to cover certain news stories'.

His colleague, Ali Al Amoudi, a senior journalist for *Al Ittihad* who covered the civil war in Somalia and published a book entitled *Al Qarn Al Afriqi* (The horn of Africa) on his experiences as a war correspondent, had a similar point of view: 'For instance, when there is a public event at night that requires coverage by a journalist, the chief editor would select a male journalist instead of a female journalist out of decency and decorum, although female journalists will not hesitate in taking the initiative to cover public events at night or even to travel on a mission abroad'.

From this perspective, the assignment of tasks to Emirati female journalists on the basis of what is deemed socially acceptable was a norm that I personally observed in the male-dominated newsrooms in Dubai and Abu Dhabi, even though the current chief editor in Dubai is female. In one conversation I had with a male senior editor in Dubai, where only two Emirati women work as field reporters, he said: 'Because of their nature and out of fear for their safety, we tend not to send Emirati female journalists to cover news of accidents, let alone fires or wars, while men, regardless of their age, take the risk and may be killed eventually'. Emirati men's attitudes towards and treatment of Emirati women inside the newsroom reflect the depth of such traditional attitudes towards women.

However, there is a group of journalists—both Emirati and Arab, both male and female—who feel that the media sector in the Emirates is not gendered, based on their positive interactions with each other and the fact that the top leadership openly works to empower Emirati women and ensure their integration in the media sector to contribute to the country's development. For example, Fatema Al Senani, head of production for ADMC, said that she receives 'complete support and trust in my capabilities from my employer. The leadership too supports the emancipation of Emirati women in the media sector'. She stated that in the preceding three years, ADMC 'hired three Emirati female executive directors, 15 division heads, and 20 supervisors. All are Emirati females'.

Mona Al Hmoudi, who works as an investigator for *Al Ittihad*, believes that the media sector is not male-dominated at all and that the work environment is stimulating. She said:

> Male and female journalists work together in harmony as one team, and I often play the role of the team leader bossing male journalists around when we are required to cover a conference or an event. They would receive orders to accomplish a certain task from me directly without complaint. My male colleagues are competent, mindful of the teamwork spirit, and do not compete negatively with their female colleagues. Our work ethics increase motivation, and my male colleagues trust my professional judgment.... Everything here is offered equally in respect to salaries and training courses.

Hana Al Hamadi, a senior journalist at *Al Ittihad*, is known amongst her colleagues for writing bold features about marital infidelity, abortion, foster parents, and imprisoned female drug addicts. She similarly declared:

> The media industry is not male-dominated. Men and women work together like bees in a hive, because at the end of the day, we all represent the newspaper. In addition, the male senior editor of our division never misses an opportunity to express his appreciation for our success in covering news stories during staff meetings. There is no such discrimination in terms of the working hours, the distribution of work shifts, and receiving training courses.

Moza Fikri, who became the first Emirati female digital media managing editor at *Al Bayan*, is very loyal to her workplace, which she joined in 1996. She is grateful to both the newspaper's executive management and the governing leadership for empowering Emirati women in the media sector. She proudly stated, 'I haven't faced any challenges in dealing with my male chief editors and directors.... I have witnessed several organizational changes inside the corporation and dealt with different male directors, who have treated me with total respect. We live in a country that empowers women and champion women's emancipation in the workplace'.

Shamsa Saif Al Hanaee, who became the first and youngest female sports reporter at *Al Ittihad*, for which she launched a weekly supplement on women's sports, thinks that the working environment at the paper reflects gender equality at every level, even in terms of salaries and promotions. She explained:

> Everyone working here is cooperative; even male sources who I interview are cooperative too. They are impressed by the fact that an Emirati female reporter is present to cover their activities; they always say that to me. Looking at my current status and tasks, I think that I'm being paid fairly.... We work as one team here, like a family. When I am absent on medical leave, for instance, my male colleague would volunteer to cover an event on my behalf, then write the feature and publish it under my full name. I do the same for them.

With a postdoctorate degree in international law from the Paris-Sorbonne University in Abu Dhabi, Abdulla Abdulkarim, a senior editor of economic news for *Al Bayan*, appreciates women's presence in the journalistic field but admits that he envies Emirati women for all the support they receive from the country's leadership and from the executive management at local entities, including the newspaper. He said, 'There is no gender inequality in the media industry or any other industry in the Emirates. Women receive complete support, and we as men are jealous of that! ... I don't really care if the editor-in-chief is male or female as long as they are professional and sufficiently skilled'.

Remarkably, Salam Abu Shihab, a Palestinian who works as the manager of the *Al Khaleej* newspaper office in Abu Dhabi, prefers to hire female instead of male journalists. He explained:

> I honestly prefer appointing female journalists because they are more determined and productive than male journalists. Female journalists engage more effectively with the public and write influential features on community-related causes, and naturally, female journalists are more sensitive and emotional; you can see that through their writings. They are more human in the sense that they write from the heart, giving any cause huge importance and significance.

A.D., a Palestinian business reporter for *Al Khaleej*, doesn't mind working closely with female journalists, even if he receives a lower salary than them. He admitted:

> My female colleague receives a higher salary than me, although we started working at the newspaper in the same year, but it didn't make me feel discriminated against. I know for a fact that her work is outstanding because her Arabic language is stronger than mine, and she has a master's degree too. Hard work pays off, I think.

Conclusion

The findings of this chapter underscore the universality of women journalists' experiences with gender disparity, the glass ceiling, sexism, and negative stereotypes in the Emirates and elsewhere. When it comes to the number of Emirati women in the media and their journalistic roles specifically, however, there is a lack of reliable statistics. I was not able to access such information either in the newsrooms or from official government sources. What has been verified to date is that the number of Emirati journalists who are members of the UAE Journalists' Association reached 137 in 2021.[12] Three of these are females who have been appointed board members of the association's council: Fadhila Al Muaini, Hessa Saif, and Salama Al Ketbi.[13] In 2017, a survey revealed that '60.8 percent of the working journalists in the Emirates are Arab expatriates from the Middle East, while 28.7 percent of the working journalists are Emiratis', who reported that 'journalism and media are not attractive fields for locals due to social reasons and low salaries'.[14]

For the past three decades, following the country's political independence in 1971, Emirati women have been underrepresented in the field of journalism due to gender politics, gendered stereotypes, and male dominance. During a lecture on women in journalism in 2004, Aisha Sultan, an Emirati columnist for the Dubai Arabic daily newspaper *Al Bayan*, stated that the media is a challenging field for 'Arab women in general, and Gulf women in particular, because of the biased male mentality that seeks to marginalise the effective role of women in the profession of journalism'.[15]

Notes

1 Al Malki et al. (2012, p. 112).
2 Ibid., p. 12.
3 Mitra (2014).
4 Darwish (2009, p. 285).
5 Ibid., p. 286.
6 *Cairo Scene* (2016).
7 Better known in the Middle East as a *keffiyeh*, the *ghutra* is a long traditional garment used by men in the Arab Gulf countries to cover the head and shoulders as part of their traditional day-to-day clothing. It is tied to the head with a black piece of cord, known as an *aghal*.
8 Arab Media Forum (2014).
9 Al Malki et al. (2012).
10 A prominent Iraqi Kurd, who served as vice president of Iraq from March 1991 to the fall of Saddam Hussein in April 2003.
11 Mouzah Matar was elected president of the mooted Women's Media Group in Dubai in 2001. The proposed group, presented to the Dubai Press Club with the aim of fostering solidarity amongst Arab female journalists, was never, in fact, launched as an official organization.
12 Al Malki et al. (2012).
13 Abdul Raouf (2021).
14 Darwish (2009).
15 *Khaleej Times* (2004).

References

Abdul Raouf, S. (2021). 'Election of the Board of Directors of the Emirati Journalists Association'. *Al Etihad News Center*. Available at: https://www.aletihad.ae [Accessed 21 June 2023].

Al Malki, A., Kaufer, D., Ishizaki, S. and Dreher, K. (2012). *Arab Women in Arab News*. New York, NY: Bloomsbury Publishing.

Arab Media Forum. (2014). *Are Television Channels Attracting Viewers with Beauty over Brains?* Available at: http://www.arabmediaforum.ae/en/media-center/press-releases/are-television-channels-attracting-viewers-with-beauty-over-brains.aspx [Accessed 28 August 2017].

Cairo Scene. (2016). 'Egyptian TV Banning Female Presenters for Being Fat?' 11 August. Available at: http://www.cairoscene.com/Buzz/Fat-Women-Are-Not-Allowed-On-Egyptian-State-Television [Accessed 6 September 2017].

Darwish, A. (2009). *Social Semiotics of Arabic Satellite Television*. Melbourne, Australia: Writescope Pty.

Khaleej Times. (2004). 'Call for Greater Role for Women in Journalism'. 8 March. Available at: https://www.khaleejtimes.com/nation/general/call-for-greater-role-for-women-in-journalism [Accessed 17 September 2017].

Mitra, B., Webb, M. and Wolfe, C. (2014). 'Audience Responses to the Physical Appearance of Television Newsreaders'. *Participations*, 11(2), pp. 45–57.

6 Journalists at Odds over Censorship, Language, and PR Influence

Based on my observations and interviews, I discovered that Emirati newsrooms are engulfed by censorship. There are censorship and content divisions in place at every media corporation that are responsible for monitoring the news broadcasts and publication of news features. I also found that the Emirati male and female journalists that I interviewed and observed routinely practice self-censorship, as do the expat Arabs and other foreigners, who constitute over 80 percent of the journalistic corps in the country, as documented by Kirat in his study of journalism in the Emirates in 2004,[1] yielding a silenced media that does not report transparently on issues crucial to Emirati society.

The dominance of censorship and self-censorship as non-gendered newsroom practices in the Emirates has impacted the journalistic skills and output of journalists generally. As a result of the limitations on their freedom of expression and the inhibition of a free press, the Emirates ranked 138th out of 180 countries in Reporters Without Borders' World Press Freedom Index.[2] As I observed Dubai's *Akhbar Al Emarat* and Abu Dhabi's *Oloum Al Dar* teams and interviewed their members for this book, I realised that they seemed to be aware of the red lines, or the so-called triangle, related to the main three taboo subjects: religion, politics, and sex. Unlike the early generation of pioneer journalists who created the golden era of the Emirati press by publishing bold news stories from the 1970s into the 1990s, some of the new generation seemed to be unaware of the penal codes of the media law, which date back to 1980. They are confident in the practice of self-censorship, believing it saves them from trouble and helps them produce news that is in keeping with the country's agenda. A few were frustrated about the current media situation, but they did nothing to change it. For example, any bold features that they proposed were eventually sidelined, as the following testimonials reveal.

Using a pseudonym to hide her real identity, Mahra, who graduated from the college of journalism at Baghdad University in Iraq and worked as a reporter and editor for two Emirati magazines in the late 1970s, believes that the censorship rules in the Emirates during the early 1980s were not clearly identified by the censors and local authorities. While well aware of the sensitive religious and cultural

DOI: 10.4324/9781003488415-6

norms in the Emirates, journalists often found the standards for censoring their work to be random and absurd. She recalled:

> Most of the time, we weren't aware of the nature of the editorial or pictorial content that censors might delete; they just didn't tell us, it wasn't clear, so we ended up having paragraphs deleted or an entire edition of the magazine censored. One time, a censor deleted a picture—it was a painting by Picasso—because it reveals a woman's bosoms, he said!

She continued, 'All journalists practised self-censorship inside the newsroom, and we used to receive censors from the Ministry of Information and Culture,[3] who would review the editorial and pictorial contents of our magazine—every edition—before it went to print'.

Mohamed Al Hammadi, the editor-in-chief of *Al Ittihad* newspaper, tried to convince me that self-censorship is a professional practice. He said:

> Naturally, editors-in-chief practise censorship. At the end of the day, they must have a point of view. Everyone practises self-censorship and that is part of the profession, in which you need to understand why you write and when to publish, because that's what matters. For instance, when we face a setback in our relationship with Iran, we would write to criticize their political attitude, but when both sides decide to set a round-table meeting with the aim of solving matters, we should not write to condemn them again because the timing is wrong. Another thing, we should never associate censorship with fear because a writer must be bold and courageous enough to write; yet again, what is important for a writer is to understand when to be bold and when to write.

Al Hammadi, whose book *Khareef Al Ikhwan* (The autumn of the Muslim brotherhood) was published in 2017, writes political columns and specialises in the history of Islamic extremism and the Muslim Brotherhood. He was a member of the press freedom committee at both the UAE Journalists' Association and the Arab and Middle Eastern Journalists' Association. Asked for his opinion of the 1980 media law, he replied, 'The current law is 40 years old and the world is changing 180 degrees. I wrote an article on this subject when the FNC[4] decided to examine the current law and propose a new one. Their proposal[5] for the new media law was appalling and does not strengthen the media's role'.

In a brief conversation with an editor for *Oloum Al Dar* news broadcast at Abu Dhabi News Centre, who preferred to remain anonymous, I asked about his knowledge of media law. He said, 'I know the restrictions. Of course, it exists. There's no freedom of the press. We're a tool aimed at promoting the government's initiatives. We don't practise investigative reporting'. While we were talking, the director of the news centre was giving a tour of the newsroom to an executive Emirati guest. We both paused, and I wondered whether the editor had done so out of fear of talking openly. When I asked him if this was the case, he replied vehemently, 'Of course not, because he knows exactly what I'm talking about. He is aware of the oppressive media structure. I don't hide anything'.

This young Emirati editor believes that he has the right to express his opinion openly as an individual. However, the current media law, described as draconian by Human Rights Watch, restricts his right to free expression as a journalist and does not protect journalism as a profession. Under article 42 of the law, for instance, a journalist may be 'imprisoned for a term no less than six months',[6] or 'pay a fine no less than 1,000 dirhams and no more than 10,000 dirhams, if prohibited content was published, and the court may suspend the activity of the newspaper'.[7]

The courts have been involved on various occasions. In 2009, for instance, the Dubai-based Arabic daily newspaper *Al Emarat Al Youm* had its licence suspended for 20 days as a result of an accusation of libel. The editor-in-chief, Sami Al Riyami, and the publisher, Abdul Latif Al Sayegh, were each fined 20,000 dirhams. Three years earlier, the paper published an article alleging that Warsan Stables used performance-enhancing steroids on its horses in advance of a race in Abu Dhabi.[8] Before that, on 2 February 1987, the Abu Dhabi-based Arabic daily newspaper *Al Fajir* was suspended for two weeks after publishing an article criticising what it called the lack of unity in the federation.[9]

In response to the low press-freedom rankings given by international organisations like Human Rights Watch, the Committee to Protect Journalists (CPJ), and Freedom House to the Emirates (Freedom House, for instance, ranked the UAE 137th out of 196 countries in 2008),[10] the National Media Council (NMC) issued a new draft of the media law to the Federal National Council (FNC) in January 2009.[11] However, the UAE Journalists' Association rejected it because it consisted of 45 articles that restricted media freedom, including ten articles on penalties and punishments for journalists who violated its clauses.[12] The CPJ wrote a grievance letter to the UAE President about the draft, asking him to disapprove of it.[13] Aside from the overt legal regime, Emirati authorities compel newspapers to publish news stories that promote the government's achievements and interfere in newspapers' production through both written and unwritten orders, transmitted by top officials to the newspapers' administrations.[14] Further, the same political powers control the appointment of the newspapers' administrative board and editorial staff to ensure their loyalty to the government.[15]

In this context, journalists have developed an obeisant press that promotes national cohesion and loyalty to the country and its leadership. There is little support for investigative journalism in the newsrooms, where the press is considered 'a tool to promote the government's initiatives, and used only to act as a backbone to defend their image and reputation from damage by external forces'.[16]

This was evident when I observed the national news broadcasts at both news centres as well as other local news centres[17] across the seven Emirates. I observed how editors for Dubai's *Akhbar Al Emarat*[18] and Abu Dhabi's *Oloum Al Dar*[19] compete daily to produce influential national news reports, with continuous attempts to get exclusive coverage of an event or a statement from a member of the ruling family, a member of the ministerial cabinet when a major conference is held, or a state visit. The daily tasks inside the Dubai and Abu Dhabi newsrooms are dominated by repetition and routine. Both teams start by editing a long list of press releases, government statements, and a collection of official photographs and videos often developed by press editors and camera crews working for the country's official news agency (WAM) and the Security Media, which is run by the Ministry of Interior.[20] News reports are thus controlled and pre-written in a certain language and format that are dictated by the authorities, and censorship is effectively omnipresent.

The journalists interviewed for this study acknowledged the reality of media and journalism practice in the Emirates. Some reflected on it as an exercise of patriotic journalism, in which they produce responsible news material to make the public aware of and secure from external threats, while others admitted that this specific reality has divorced them from engaging in true journalism and playing the role of watchdogs, which is not recognised in the Emirates, as explained in Chapter 4. Fatema Al Senani, for instance, stressed how local media corporations serve the government:

> We need to understand a very important issue: as Abu Dhabi television, our role is to support the government's mission. We consider ourselves as a tool of the government. Freedom of practise should be in parallel with the government's mission. We should refrain from broadcasting things that may cause negative reactions or retaliation. The media should follow the government's mission and support it. In the end, you don't work to harm your nation.

Meanwhile, Al Hammadi believes that the Emirati media is an instrument well-tuned for people's enlightenment.[21] He stated:

> I think that the media environment in the Emirates is quite fair and I would describe it as a developed media that runs in parallel with the development of the country. Writers can criticize and express their points of view freely, but responsibly, by presenting proofs and so on. This practise reflects the media culture in the Emirates. I wrote a column in 2000 criticizing the Council of Ministers for renewing the terms of ministers who had served in their positions in the cabinet for almost twenty years. The column was entitled 'How Long Will They Stay?' And it was published in the official government newspaper, *Al Ittihad*.

Salam Abu Shihab, who spent 33 years writing investigative features on healthcare, also believes that practising self-censorship reflects a journalist's sense of responsibility and professionalism and that press freedom in the Emirates is high. He said, 'In the UAE, we are not controlled and our work is not censored. There is absolute freedom to write about anything. Self-censorship is a practise that a journalist obeys to determine whether the topic written will serve the society in the first place'.

Just like the older generation of Emirati journalists, the younger generation is keen on working hard to give back and contribute to the nation's development by supporting the leadership and the federal union, preserving its values and heritage, and passing them on to their children. The younger generation of Emiratis wants to show their patriotism and loyalty to their country and monarchy and to protect its reputation from harm. Mona Al Hmoudi said:

> In *Al Ittihad* newspaper, we don't allow journalists to fish in troubled waters with the aim of destroying the country's image and reputation. And if we shed light on a negative case, we constantly ensure that we offer solutions for it. When you read the terms and conditions of the media law, you realize that it does not restrict your work as a journalist. But there is a level of illegality, so we don't cross the red lines like writing about religion and the divine entity for instance.

Abdulla Abdulkarim expressed a similar view of 'responsible' journalism:

> During the annual meeting of media professionals with Sheikh Mohammed bin Rashid, which I attended to represent the newspaper, he urged us to develop an enlightening media. Journalism is the fourth estate and must be practised responsibly. I practise journalism responsibly and understand the impact of words on people. I practise self-censorship and will not write topics that conflict with the national agenda. *Al Bayan* … will never publish news stories that would harm national security or the country's reputation.

He added:

> If I were to measure the level of *Al Bayan*'s freedom since its launch 35 years ago, I would say it has changed rapidly for the better. Just like your situation now, from a social perspective, women in the past were not allowed to travel abroad alone to pursue an academic degree, but now the society has become quite open towards this change and to women's equality.

Arab expat journalists interviewed for this book, however, provided divergent opinions on the position of the media in the Emirates relative to the other Arab states from which they have come. They reported that in those places, the media environment is either even more severely oppressed, putting journalists under constant psychological pressure and fear of the authorities, or freer, providing a far more liberating journalistic experience. For instance, Muna Saeed Al Taher, an Iraqi field reporter for *Al Roeya* newspaper, believes that the media law and application of censorship in the Emirates are fair and that she never felt threatened in comparison to Iraq, where journalists were under 'intellectual siege', as she put it. She explained:

> We write within the space given to us, and inside each journalist lives a policeman that practises self-censorship. I come from an oppressive school

and lived in a dictatorship. We are guests in this country; that is why we don't reveal the negative side of its society in an unpleasant way in writing, but rather in a polite way. After all, an ideal society does not exist. In Iraq, we lived under a dictatorship, with no freedom of expression.

While Yousef Bustangi believes that press freedom is high in Jordan, where he previously worked, as reflected by the growing emphasis on investigative journalism there, the picture is different in the Emirates:

Journalism practised here is very progressive, in terms of using new technologies for publishing, especially now with the emergence of digital media. The Emirates has strong economic and technological infrastructures. However, in terms of the editorial content, protocol-driven news controls public opinion and journalistic practises.

The priority of news coverage goes to the government and its rulers for one particular reason only: the government and rulers are the decision makers here, and their news has a massive influence on the public's lives. It is, therefore, natural that journalistic practise reflects this cultural reality. Journalism in Jordan as a field doesn't possess a developed technological infrastructure, but in terms of practise, it possesses freedom of writing and expression, that's for sure.

The PR agencies: The new hegemonic

Apart from the official censorship imposed on and the excessive self-censorship exercised by male and female journalists in the Emirates, regardless of their nationality, my observations and interviews revealed another non-gendered influence on newsroom norms: the rise of PR agencies in the Emirates, affecting news production, the relationship between journalists and external sources, and journalistic practice in general.

The growth of the advertising industry in the mid-1980s, due to the expansion of newspaper and magazine publication and the increase in television audiences, led to a spike in international PR agencies' presence in the Emirates.[22] These included Pan Gulf PR, Bain Euro RSCG, Gulf Hill and Knowlton, and Headline PR, which established offices in Dubai and Abu Dhabi. Up to 63 percent of government departments and semi-governmental and private entities in the country have established in-house public relations departments to market and manage external communications with the local media using the expertise of these international agencies.[23]

Through the interviews that I conducted, I discovered that the relationship between journalists and PR agents could be cooperative and helpful, but for the most part, it is characterised by conflicts and misunderstandings over the collection of information and communication with sources. As a result, the presence of over 100 international PR agencies in the country, as reported by the Middle East Public Relations Associations (MEPRA) in 2021,[24] has debilitated journalists' motivation to produce hard-edged and exclusive news stories. J.M., 55, an Emirati reporter for WAM, said:

> The spread of PR agencies added restraints to journalists' work, and in some areas, it has affected our competence and ability to produce influential news. Now, officials refuse to talk or to give us a short statement, asking that we wait for the publication of the official press release. Even if I manage to interview an official, who would cooperate with me out of respect and trust for my long career experience, I find that the exact statement has already been published as a quote in the PR agency's press release.

Tubeileh has encountered similar obstacles in dealing with local sources. She said:

> In the past, I used to contact any source directly, even if this source is a minister. However, now, I need to work with a PR agency to get the information needed. In the Emirates, the environment is completely different. I would either work with the PR agency or wait for an official entity to release a statement through its press office.

Agreeing with her *Al Ittihad* colleague's point of view, Badria Al Kassar stated:

> In the past, we used to visit local entities to interview senior officials, writing their statements using simple tools like a pen and a notebook, or recording it with a voice recorder. Now, we need to communicate with PR agencies to schedule an interview for us with the local source, and we have to submit the list of questions to them. We don't practise journalism professionally any more.

For Jalila, the overwhelming presence of PR agencies is creating a major crisis in journalism in the Emirates:

> I see them as a dam that creates barriers between officials and journalists, because it is prohibited for us to receive information without their consent. Such barriers resulted in tepidness; journalism as a profession is no longer real and competition is absent among newspapers because PR agencies have unified all news stories delivered to us, which has resulted in a lack of excellence in practise, and in the lack of finding the scoop for journalists.

Reda El Bawardy, a senior Egyptian field reporter for *Al Roeya* newspaper, feels that journalism has turned into 'penal labour', now more than ever, given PR agencies' power. Alsayed Salama, an Egyptian senior journalist for *Al Ittihad*, believes that it is the deficiency of academic programmes in media and journalists' focus on emerging media platforms that is primarily to blame for media corporations' complete dependence on the PR industry: 'I think that the strong presence of PR agencies, as intermediaries, has occurred due to the journalists' weakness in practising journalism professionally'.

Fussha: The loss of classical Arabic in the newsroom

While observing the live national news broadcasts in the Abu Dhabi and Dubai newsrooms, I discovered that Emirati news anchors, and sometimes field reporters, were weak at reading *Fussha* (Classical Arabic) fluently to deliver the news. This was especially true of the younger generation, in comparison with the more experienced Emirati news anchors of the 1970s and 1980s. The younger generation depends fully on the news scripts written by linguist editors, mostly Arab expats from Egypt and Palestine, who are experienced in writing news scripts in the *Fussha* format. But even though news scripts are written with diacritics that also appear on the teleprompter, I observed Emirati news anchors making errors of pronunciation on a daily basis. On one occasion, during a live broadcast from inside the Dubai newsroom, I observed an Emirati female news anchor reading the list of questions written for her for a phone interview with an MP. During the two-minute live conversation, she was entirely dependent on the chief editor, who provided her with instructions on how to cut the MP's answers short through an earpiece, with interjections like 'It's evident, thank you', or 'Yes', or 'Briefly please'.

Most of the young news anchors have studied mass media at university in the English language, meaning they are fluent in reading the news script in English. This is something that I witnessed inside the Dubai newsroom, where a subchannel uses the same studio to broadcast local news for its non-Arabic-speaking viewers. On one occasion, a young male Emirati news anchor appeared on set wearing a traditional dress and started reading the news script in perfect English with an American accent. When I commented on the Arabic-language issues amongst Emirati news anchors, a senior editor in the Dubai newsroom said:

Today, we deal with the 'OMG' generation. Unfortunately, there is a common weakness in practising Classical Arabic among the young Emirati TV presenters, due to a lack of interest in reading Arabic literature, or in understanding the language's complex grammar. The older generation of TV presenters [from the 1970s and 1980s] paid attention to the practise and vocalization of Classical Arabic, in comparison with today's TV presenters, who seem distracted by various things, especially when they are on air, like their image in front of the camera and on the television screen.

While observing the live news broadcasts at both newsrooms, I noticed that the on-air elocution of Emirati news anchors is weak. On day four of observing the newsroom activities at Abu Dhabi News Centre, I specifically documented the linguistic mistakes of a female news host (who also repeatedly adjusted her headscarf while reading from the teleprompter during the live broadcast, causing the microphone to buzz). When I shared this observation with an Egyptian senior editor sitting next to me in the gallery, he commented, 'It is a common weakness among young Emirati news hosts and field reporters, in particular, to master Arabic elocution despite our efforts in training them in-house'.

Another problem I observed amongst Emirati news anchors and field reporters alike was their use of colloquial Arabic, particularly during live phone conversations with guests at the news studio or while conducting live interviews with officials at local events. This rising phenomenon could be devastating for the Arabic-speaking world, where Arab media journalists use colloquial language, or *aammiyya* (slang), or what is known as *Arabizi* (colloquial Arabic written using English letters), on every platform, print, broadcast, and digital. Analysing the rise of *aammiyya*, May Zaki, a teacher of linguistics at the American University of Sharjah, argued that this shift from using Classical Arabic is linked with recent campaigns across the Arab world, from North Africa to the Middle East and the Gulf, to strengthen nationalism through the promotion of *aammiyya* in film production, talk shows, and advertising in particular, as a new form of political identity, to distinguish between them as nations with unique cultures and political histories.[25]

The use of colloquial Arabic is now fairly commonplace amongst print and broadcast journalists in the Emirates, and with the emergence of social media platforms and lexical innovations like emojis to express feelings, Emirati journalists prefer to use *aammiyya* when posting online. A number of pioneering Emirati intellectuals have shared their dismay about the absence of Classical Arabic in the local media. Ali Abu Al Reesh, a novelist and columnist for *Al Ittihad* newspaper, warned that it 'will result in further alienation and diversion between Arabs'.[26]

The Emirati female columnist Fadheela Al Muaini, who writes for *Al Bayan* newspaper in Dubai, has blamed the increasing use of *aammiyya* in journalism in part on editors 'who no longer bother to revise and amend articles before publishing them in the newspaper'.[27] However, Nasser Al Dhaheri, an Emirati columnist for *Al Ittihad* newspaper, has argued that the 'use of *aammiyya* is often misunderstood and that it should never be taken as opposed to the use of Classical Arabic language in the media', but rather as an addition to any journalistic feature that has a 'local peculiarity', in which a journalist, including himself, could use *aammiyya* as a joke or a form of black comedy.[28]

Conclusion

The observations and semi-structured interviews with 40 Emirati and Arab expat journalists revealed the nature of media practice and culture in the Emirates, where freedom of expression is overwhelmed by self-censorship because of socio-political influences that force journalists to act cautiously and the outdated media law replete with oppressive regulations that diminish journalists' rights.

Nevertheless, the media is relatively well developed in the Emirates for two reasons. First, the generous financial support that the print and broadcast outlets receive from the government to cover employee costs offers Emirati journalists, in particular, good benefits, career development plans, and opportunities for promotion since HR departments adhere to the process of Emiratisation.[29] Second, the emergence of digital media has created a diversified media environment. Every print and broadcast media outlet in the country has now developed multiple digital media platforms, from social media accounts to websites designed for outreach to the local community, providing up-to-date news stories in seconds with appealing photographs and videos.

Media development, however, has also created challenges in the profession of journalism. Emirati and Arab expat journalists are isolated within their cubicles inside the newsroom, playing the role of couriers, receiving news from official channels or PR agencies and firms, rather than going out into the field to report news and interview sources directly. The content of the print and broadcast news in the Emirates is loyal, patriotic, repetitive, and promotional—marketing the government's initiatives and achievements in the absence of investigative journalism and press freedom. These non-gendered newsroom practices attest to the government's authority over news production, driven by its fear that unfettered journalism would yield unflattering images of the state. Its dominance is reflected in protocol-driven and criticism-free news, which journalists produce in fear for their own security, which is not guaranteed by the current media law of the UAE.

Notes

1 Kirat (2004).
2 Reporters Without Borders (2021).
3 The Ministry of Information and Culture was replaced in 2006 by the National Media Council (NMC). The NMC was in turn replaced in March 2023 by the current UAE Media Council.
4 The UAE's Federal National Council.
5 The proposal was not approved, and the country still uses the 40-year-old media law.
6 UAE Federal Government (1980).
7 Ibid.
8 Morris (2009).
9 Jones (2001, p. 2498).
10 Gulf News (2008).
11 Deibert (2010, pp. 591–592).
12 Deibert (2010).
13 Ibid.
14 BuMetea (2013, p. 25).
15 BuMetea (2013).
16 Rugh (2004, p. 65).
17 In the northern emirates, there are a number of media corporations, such as Sharjah Media Corporation (which operates four cable channels and two Arabic-speaking radio stations), Ajman Independent Studio (for television and radio production), and Fujairah Media Group (which operates two cable channels and four radio stations, of which two are dedicated to Asian expats).
18 The *Akhbar Al Emarat* team consists of 15 Emirati members, including five female editors, of whom three work as news anchors and field reporters jointly.
19 The *Oloum Al Dar* team consists of 18 Emirati members, with ten males working as news anchors, editors, and field reporters jointly, and eight females working as news anchors, two females as field reporters, and four females as editors and producers.

20 The Security Media is a media department operated by the Ministry of Interior. It was established in 2008 to act as the governmental communication arm of the Ministry of Interior and Abu Dhabi Police.
21 'Enlightening media' is a term often used by journalists interviewed in this book. In this context, it is a form of media ethics that relates to journalistic practice in the Emirates, where journalists practise 'responsible reporting' to highlight news that is relevant to the public interest and the improvement of government services. The practice also dictates that journalists avoid the invasion of other people's privacy and instill distinctive Emirati social values to preserve national cohesion and maintain the country's political and economic stability.
22 Kirat (2005).
23 Ibid.
24 Middle East Public Relations Association (2020).
25 Kirat (2005).
26 Juma (2013).
27 Ibid.
28 Ibid.
29 Emiratisation is a process that seeks to replace a reliance on foreign expatriate workers with UAE nationals. It involves not only recruiting UAE nationals but also training them to acquire the skills and competencies for the assigned work.

References

BuMetea, A. (2013). *Political Communication in the Arabian Gulf Countries*. Bloomington, IN: Xlibris LLC.
Deibert, R. (2010). *Access Controlled: The Shaping of Power, Rights, and Rule in Cyberspace*. Cambridge, MA: MIT Press.
Jones, D. (2001). *Censorship*. New York, NY: Routledge.
Juma, A. (2013). 'Colloquial Dialect Pursues Formal Arabic in the Media'. *Al Ittihad*. Translated by the author. 19 June. Available at: http://www.alittihad.ae/details.php?id=59099&y=2013&article=full [Accessed 6 June 2017].
Kirat, M. (2004). 'A Profile of Women Journalists in the United Arab Emirates'. *Journal of International Communication*, 10(1), pp. 54–78.
Kirat, M. (2005). 'Public Relations in the United Arab Emirates: The Emergence of a Profession'. *Science Direct*. 29 May. Available at: https://www.academia.edu/22261294/Public_relations_in_the_United_Arab_Emirates_The_emergence_of_a_profession [Accessed 8 May 2017].
Middle East Public Relations Association. (2020). *Registered Agencies*. MEPRA. Available at: https://www.mepra.org/membership/registered-agencies/ [Accessed 13 June 2023].
Morris, L. (2009). 'Emarat Al Youm Back in Print'. *The National*. 27 July. Available at: http://www.thenational.ae/news/uae-news/emarat-al-youm-back-in-print [Accessed 13 June 2017].
Reporters Without Borders. (2021). *2021 World Press Freedom Index*. Available at: https://rsf.org/en/2021-world-press-freedom-index-journalism-vaccine-against-disinformation-blocked-more-130-countries [Accessed 4 August 2022].
UAE Federal Government. (1980). *Federal Law No. 15 for 1980 Concerning Publications and Publishing*. Abu Dhabi: Ministry of Information and Culture.

7   Tribalism and the Female Journalist's Voice

A Dilemma Overlooked

In the Emirates, historically, women were next to invisible in journalism. They were rarely seen working in the field, in contrast to their female counterparts elsewhere. Even after the discovery of oil and the expansion of the education system, the fields of print and broadcast media have still proven to be very difficult for Emirati women to enter. This is because the patriarchal society still views the media industry as unrespectable and shameful for Emirati women to pursue as an academic focus and as a profession.

Any attempt by Emirati women to depart from ancient traditional practices and tribal customs remains difficult and is still viewed by the patriarchs as against the principles of Islam. Emirati women still endure segregation and veiling, which are often imposed by societal pressures rather than adopted as a personal choice. They are also obliged to behave 'properly' and to appear modest to protect their tribe's honour and reputation. Female journalists in many other Western and Eastern societies, including those of the rest of the Middle East and North Africa (MENA), do not have to endure these gendered societal restrictions, which are embedded in the tribal culture of the Emirati and other Arab Gulf societies. This has allowed the media elsewhere to see it as a meaningful academic major and a respectable profession for women to pursue.

The complex notion of tribal belonging, which obliges Arab Gulf women to submit to suffocating rules, determines the course of their private and public lives. Tribal belonging is not predominant in most other MENA region societies, which have adapted to the historical waves of social change and progress in the context of postcolonial modernisation and postmodern globalisation. This has resulted in the fading of tribalism in its ancient form, as it is still practised religiously by today's societies in the Arab Gulf states.

In a survey conducted for *Al Aan TV* by YouGov, nearly 20 percent of Emirati women expressed an interest in working in the print and broadcast media. However, nearly 30 percent of Emirati men who were surveyed objected to the idea of their female relatives writing in newspapers or appearing on television due to cultural sensitivities related to tribal customs, particularly tribal belonging.[1]

In this context, what does the concept of tribal belonging encompass? Why is it viewed as a central pillar in the construction of Emirati society? And how have

DOI: 10.4324/9781003488415-7

tribal belonging and the quest for preserving tribal hegemony impacted women journalists in the Emirates specifically? To apprehend Emirati social structure and its effect on journalistic practice, in this chapter, I examine how gender as an identity marker intersects with other markers such as tribe, family, and class in the Emirates. I reveal the findings in which the Emirati journalists interviewed for this book conveyed their perspectives on the dominance of what Palestinian intellectual Hisham Sharabi described as 'tribal patriarchalism', which has proved adamantly resistant to change.[2]

Interpretations of tribal belonging

Within Emirati society, as in many Arab Gulf states, tribal belonging is 'intertwined with tribal identity, which engages with aspects of kinship, hierarchy, loyalty and values'.[3] Following in their ancestral footsteps, Emiratis 'define their identity first by bloodlines and then geographically'.[4] This form of identity has been associated—in broader geographical terms—with what has been called 'the belt of classic patriarchy', which is 'characterized by male domination, son preference, restrictive codes of behavior for women, and the association of family honor with female virtue. In the Muslim areas of the patriarchal belt … veiling and sex segregation, legitimated on the basis of the Quran or [prophetic] hadith, form part of the gender system'.[5]

This set of values and norms, shared amongst the oil-rich Arab Gulf societies, has resulted in an internal class stratification that is kinship-oriented. This class stratification is based on tribal descent and on specific tribes' political and economic history, creating an internal social division in which Emiratis 'consider the mental divide between tribal and non-tribal groups, arguing that this man is from this lineage, my relatives belong to another lineage, and this family is not even tribal. People of different tribal background might work and live together, but they still respect the invisible line that separates them from the "other" and regulates or limits any interaction'.[6]

With sweeping social changes, the impact of phenomena such as globalisation and economic development, and the increase of the expatriate population—which accounted for 88.52 percent of Emirati residents in 2018[7]—the mental divide has widened, affecting the relationship between Emirati nationals and the expats, despite their seemingly harmonious coexistence. As explained by Arab Gulf studies expert Frauke Heard-Bey:

> Nationals are constantly made aware of their being a minority in their own country … bringing the national population of all the seven Emirates together to form a completely undisputed class of the privileged few. In the face of the overwhelming presence of expatriates, all the genuine 'locals' perceive themselves now first and foremost as UAE citizens even though old tribal rivalries and new hierarchical discrimination continue to structure the local population internally.[8]

Apart from being burdened by societal restrictions, their minority status has also seemingly discouraged Emirati women from entering the national workforce, according to the tenth report published by the Arab Gulf States Institute in Washington (AGSIW) in 2016: 'In 2005, 1.3 million women were living in the UAE, yet only about 300,000 women were in the workforce, at least 283,000 of whom were expatriates. National women in the workforce comprised less than 3 percent of the female population'.[9]

Emirati women play a key role in maintaining the mental construct of kinship relations in both private and public through the maintenance of certain tribal customs, most notably defending the tribe's reputation and honour. This is marked by women's decorum and modesty and by their practising endogamy to protect the hegemonic social order of the Emirates' native nomadic people. The practice of endogamy, in particular, has received orthodox approval within Arab tribal societies, including those of the Arab Gulf states, which adopt the Maleki[10] interpretation of Sunni Islam in structuring Islamic jurisprudence in regards to marriage. As described by Tunisian sociologist Mounira Charrad, Islamic law, especially in its Maleki version,

> encourages kin control of marriage ties and thus facilitates both marriages within the lineage and collectively useful outside alliance. By favoring males and kin on the male side, inheritance laws solidify ties within the extended patrilineal kin group.... Maleki law defines the kin group rather than the nuclear family as the significant locus of solidarity. It facilitates and reflects the maintenance of tribal communities.[11]

This ethos produces inequalities as it limits opportunities for Emirati women. Even so, those of elite tribal backgrounds are in a better position and are often represented in state institutions as ministers of state or as executives in social, educational, environmental, or health-related organisations, thereby creating another internal societal complexity that I refer to as 'tribal exclusivity'. For example, Amal Al Qubaisi became the first female speaker of the house in the UAE's Federal National Council (FNC). Complementing her academic qualifications, she comes from one of the UAE's most prominent tribes, Al Qubaisi, long politically aligned with the ruling family. Other examples include female ministers of state, whose surnames reflect not only tribal prominence but also the fact that they have enjoyed an opulent upbringing and privileged education. This is often due to the political status of their forefathers, who served as ministers, ambassadors, or high-ranking soldiers while displaying unswerving loyalty to the monarchical system.

Tribal exclusivity in the Emirates and in the oil-rich Arab Gulf states generally has been viewed as a social deficit resulting in discrimination because of how it promotes corruption, cronyism, or *wasta*, and nepotism. Tribal exclusivity 'opposes the creation of equal citizens because only tribal members are entitled to the benefits and obliged to take the responsibilities of membership in the tribe'.[12]

Supporters of tribalism 'have failed to respond to the concerns of citizens who are not members or are members of a lower tribe or naturalised citizens. Due to this, tribalism must be seen as a form of discrimination, which stands against the notion of equality among citizens in a modern nation-state'.[13]

The social deficit caused by tribal discrimination in the Emirates was apparent in the 2019 FNC elections, where female representation was set at 50 percent by an Emiri decree and Emirati citizens were required to elect half the candidates. Observers of the voting process, including Emirati journalists, expressed their dismay when tribalism surfaced, pushing the political candidates' agendas for social change aside. Previous FNC elections[14] had demonstrated tribalism's power as a social force, with Emiratis feeling compelled to support members of their tribe as a sign of loyalty. At the 2011 polling stations, for instance, voters admitted that their votes were based on tribal affiliations. In an analysis of the 2015 election's results, *The National* newspaper reported that three of the four elected seats in Abu Dhabi went to Al Ameri tribe members, while two of the three elected seats in Ras Al Khaimah went to Al Teneiji family members, and two seats in Ajman went to Al Shamsi tribe members.[15]

Ramifications

The limited access to opportunities has become evident in the field of media, which is the focus of this book. Emirati women are underrepresented because of the dominance of tribal patriarchalism, in which any 'impurity' on the part of a woman 'is regarded as an attack on the honor of the man. In this culture, the kinship ties are so strong that the dishonorable behavior of any member of the family or tribe deeply affects all members of the tribe, and misogyny develops'.[16] This was evident in the testimonials of Emirati female journalists, who recognised the importance of media in granting them a space for self-expression and a platform to voice their concerns. This was especially important for addressing women's causes as well as granting them some sense of autonomy, despite their feeling suffocated by the misogynistic rules of tribal patriarchalism.

The following testimonials reveal the impact of tribal patriarchalism on female journalists' decision-making. Strikingly, they also reveal the impact of parental illiteracy on women's choices regarding studying and working in the print and broadcast media. More than a few of the Emirati female journalists interviewed for this book were raised by illiterate parents who received little or no education at all due to poverty and the lack of a schooling system before the discovery of oil.[17] Some enrolled in state-backed adult literacy and basic education programmes after the federal union in 1971. In addition, the testimonials reveal how Emirati society perceives the media as an industry and the members of the media community specifically.

For instance, when Rawdha decided to tell her parents about her ambition to become a journalist in 2002, she faced a harsh reaction from her mother, who was determined that her eldest daughter should major in education to become a teacher. Her father, who died in a car crash, was illiterate, while her mother completed grade six and graduated from a government-funded adult literacy and basic education programme. She remembered:

> My father supported my decision, but was worried that I might upset the authorities if I publish news features with sensitive materials. My mother, to the contrary, was so angry at me that she demotivated me at every opportunity. She used to tell me things like: 'People who join the media have a bad reputation', and 'I have raised a belly dancer!' She thought that I would remove my veil and wear indecent clothes just like those actresses she saw in black-and-white Egyptian classic movies.

Marriage and motherhood made Rawdha's position as a journalist even more challenging. She added:

> My husband is quite jealous because he dislikes the idea of me working in a mixed environment with strange men generally. He prefers segregation for women in the workplace, and he is not convinced about the boundaries that I draw for myself in the workplace to maintain decency and social decorum.

Meanwhile, Reem Al Breiki was not only prohibited from choosing journalism as a profession but, at one point, forbidden from continuing her undergraduate studies unless she chose a major that her family approved of. Eventually, she majored in history and monuments and worked as a history and social science teacher from 1999 to 2001. Pursuing her passion, however, she secretly sent columns using a pseudonym to the people's opinions section of *Al Ittihad* newspaper. She said:

> I was passionate about journalism, but due to tribal and Bedouin constraints concerning the family's name and position in the society,[18] and my mother's disapproval of journalism as a major, I couldn't study it. The stereotypes have changed, and we no longer follow what I call 'the policy of shame' or *ayeb*. Mixing with men in the same workplace was considered shameful and, therefore, was completely unacceptable.

Not only was journalism a 'no go zone' for Al Breiki, but studying at a boarding university inside the country was also likewise viewed as 'unacceptable' for female members of her tribe, who expressed fears for her safety and reputation. Families, she explained, 'began to accept this innovative student life after being introduced to the university's academic environment, which was backed by the state's support and the state's reassurance to local families regarding Emirati female students' safety. I am the first female member in the family to study at a university level'.

Mahra Al Jenaibi challenged her family by choosing to major in broadcast media at the UAE University. As an undergraduate student, she created and appeared in short documentaries, including *My Homeland*, which shed light on local tourism. As a result of her work, she won the Sheikh Majid Youth Media Award.

She said, 'I insisted in majoring in broadcast media and in participating in almost every media-related conference as an undergraduate student, defying the societal restrictions of seclusion and networking with strange men. Making personal decisions by force has eventually led my family to accept my choices'.

Yaqoutah Abdulla Al Dhanhane became emotional as she spoke about family rejection during her interview. She and her eight siblings were raised by an illiterate mother, who instilled in them the importance of education before anything else. When her parents discovered that she had abandoned her architecture major to register at a college of media, however, they

> didn't speak to me, they forbid that I write and get my full name printed in newspapers or magazines.... Gradually, my mother, a grade-six graduate, began to accept my role as a journalist. She proudly informs the neighbours each time I appear on television as a programme guest, or when my features are published in the newspaper. But my father has never changed his mind about my choice of profession to this day.

The family of Ameena Awadh Bin Amro, who earned a master's degree in media leadership, management, and marketing from the Paris-Sorbonne University in Abu Dhabi, saw her choice of profession as high-risk. She said:

> I began my career in 2005 as a columnist. I wrote a daily column entitled *Watar* [Chord] to shed light on the current regional and international political issues. For eight years, I was the only Emirati female columnist writing for the newspaper's political section. My family disapproved.... From their perspective, journalism is not a respectful profession for women, which is a common stereotype, and from a political angle, journalism brings trouble. They view it as a risky profession because journalists' rights are often unprotected.

For Leila, who interned with American and British broadcasting services before launching her professional career in 2008 writing investigative features for *The National* newspaper, the subject of stereotypes and restrictions is far more complicated. She said, 'Women cannot get away from the fact that they are still regarded by many as second-class citizens and are not considered with the same level of weight and respect given to men. I think … it's cultural, religious reasons and it's a subconscious discrimination by some—of course, not everyone'. At the end of the interview, I asked Leila if she could elaborate on her views about the impact of patriarchal and matriarchal approaches on subordinating women and oppressing feminism as an ideology in Emirati society. She responded:

> I don't like the word 'feminist' because I think it has so many negative connotations, and I don't believe that to fight for women's rights means we have to go against men.... I don't blame men for being who they are. I blame the families, I blame the culture as a whole, but am not going to

single out a man and say 'how dare you think this' because this is what his mom taught him, what his father taught him, what his grandparents taught him, what society taught him … the books he read, and religion to be honest as well, it's misinterpreted, and ignorance.

Meanwhile, Bashayer, an Emirati editor for *Al Bayan* newspaper who preferred to use a pseudonym to hide her real identity, wanted to be financially independent; she refused to stay at home after graduating from university simply because male members of her family, including her father, could take care of her needs. She did confess to me, however, that once her social status changes after marriage, she will leave the media industry for good.

Mahra did not receive support from her husband despite the fact that she had practised journalism at Baghdad University's media college, before marrying him. She said:

My husband disapproved of my choice of journalism as a career due to the long working hours, whether I was working at home or at the editorial office, and due to the fact that I travelled to distant areas and abroad to do field reporting. There was a sense of guilt too, because I left my children alone at home.

Women's submission within a patriarchal society to stereotypical gendered attributes, which cast them as the family pillars and carriers of reputable social values, is not unusual. Fedaa Mershid, an Emirati news monitor for *Al Ittihad*, had to change her work routine to accommodate her husband's wishes. She no longer accepts fieldwork and has cut down on her daily editorial office hours as well. She now supervises the pictorial content of the society supplement, which the newspaper releases every Friday and Saturday to highlight the week's most important social events. As she put it, 'Family commitments and restrictions imposed on me by my husband have changed my working habits somehow'.

Before working for a government-funded newspaper, Yusra Adil dealt with familial criticism for appearing on Baynounah TV, a private television channel in Abu Dhabi. She hosted a social talk show directed at young Emiratis, *Shababna Ghair* (Our youth is different). She said:

My grandfather, who raised me after the death of my parents, criticized me for majoring in broadcast media and considered that majoring in public relations would be more beneficial and socially appropriate for me. My family is conservative and used to criticize me for appearing on television wearing full makeup. But when I moved to work for a newspaper, they were very pleased because they thought that the elite and experts read newspapers.

Heyam Obaid Bawazir, who as an intern at CNN was trained by correspondent Jim Clancy, works today as head of news output at Abu Dhabi Television Channel One. She is the only Emirati female that I met inside the newsroom to hold such a senior position, and her colleagues have nicknamed her the 'Mother of *Oloum Al Dar*'. She started her television career in 1997 as a local field reporter, then became a foreign correspondent. Her last mission was to Palestine, where she was supposed to produce a documentary on the 1948 Palestinian exodus; the Israeli government did not release her entry pass, leaving her and the Abu Dhabi TV crew stranded at the Jordanian border. She recounted:

> My family understood the nature of my profession, but once I became a correspondent, troubles rose to the surface. They would ask me: 'How can you do this? You're a girl! How will you travel alone!' In the beginning, my brother escorted me as a guardian. My mother rejected the idea of my constant overseas tours to the extent that she didn't allow me to travel to Afghanistan.

Bawazir admitted that joining this field as an Emirati and a woman has exposed her, as well as her Emirati female counterparts, to mounting social pressures that influenced her family's opinion of the media industry. This resulted in the launch of a specific internal policy for female journalists at Abu Dhabi Media Company. She added:

> I was very enthusiastic and eager to explore every aspect of journalism. As a consequence, my working hours increased and I began to leave the newsroom late, at nine in the evening, which was seen as inappropriate for females at that time.... Everyone back home was wondering what type of tasks were keeping me occupied very late at night inside the newsroom.
>
> Familial and social pressures were far higher in Abu Dhabi at that time because patriarchy and tribalism are overemphasised in this emirate. Because of this, the [then] minister of information and culture requested executive managers at Abu Dhabi Media Company to implement a working hours' plan for female employees, under which journalistic tasks are delivered before sunset.... Male colleagues and people that we met while reporting in the field used to stare at us with disapproval.

Like Bawazir, Fatema Al Senani, who started her career as a camerawoman for Abu Dhabi television in 2007, faced multiple challenges entering the field:

> I was not the only fresh graduate—there were three other Emirati females in the newsroom, but they resigned one year later. It is difficult being a camerawoman, not only because of the daunting working hours and the physical fatigue one feels from carrying the heavy camera equipment for more than 12 hours a day, but because it is a male-dominated profession. My male colleagues would often criticize my work and question my competence. Even when I was an undergraduate student, my professor ... told me that I would never make it as a camerawoman because of my gender, tribal background, and social restraints. To survive in this environment, I had to work harder

than men to prove myself.... It was very difficult for the society to accept women's presence with strange men at the workplace, for long hours, and to see them break their seclusion. But today, you can notice the presence of Emirati women in the field, especially those who belong to prominent *asil* tribes such as Hessa Al Falasi.[19]

F.H., an Emirati presenter for Abu Dhabi Television Channel One, faced parental objections to her studying media at university level. She did manage to receive their approval after agreeing to their conditions for maintaining decorum inside the newsroom and on air. She said:

Even though my parents have studied abroad and got higher academic degrees, they were influenced by the common stereotype about the media. My parents were anxious about the negative image of celebrity TV presenters, the working environment, and the media community's reputation.... I agreed to my parents' conditions: that I create a decent style for my appearance, set a good example for Emirati girls appearing on television, and only present meaningful programmes that raise awareness on issues related to the society, the youth, and health.

The editor-in-chief of *Al Ittihad*, Mohamed Al Hammadi, agrees that social constraints still exist and that some families do not allow their daughters to work in the media sector. However, at Abu Dhabi Media Company, an internal strategy has been developed to empower Emirati female journalists. He said:

Female journalists receive an immense amount of support and appreciation in this field, especially married female journalists, because we understand that social constraints, usually imposed by husbands, may restrict them from going out into the field or travelling to cover news. At Abu Dhabi Media Company, we have appointed two Emirati females as editors-in-chief—one for *Majid*, a children's comic weekly magazine, and the other one for the *National Geographic Al Arabiya* monthly magazine. We have also appointed an Emirati female as an executive managing editor for *Zahrat Al Khaleej* women's weekly magazine, which means that Emirati females are taken into consideration when we develop the promotion list.

It sounds extreme to suggest that all Emirati women went through the same experiences and rejections to work in the media sector. From the 1960s to the 1980s, for instance, a few of the women who shaped the early wave of the journalism movement in the Emirates challenged the tribal customs by choosing to study journalism in neighbouring countries like Lebanon and Egypt, as the UAE University did not establish an academic journalism programme until 1977.[20]

As a consequence, they forced public acceptance of women's presence in the media as journalists and broadcasters who appeared without a veil and wearing Western clothes. Moreover, they appeared as TV guests debating socio-cultural issues, including Emirati women's empowerment and contributions to local arts and literature. Amongst those pioneer women is Dr. Hessa Abdullah Lootah, who wrote features on social issues in *Al Azminah Al Arabiya* (Arab times) weekly magazine. Another example is the Sharjah-born Mouzah Khamis, who wrote weekly columns in *Al Khaleej* newspaper and published special features on topics including pearl diving, herbal medicine, and agriculture in the early 1980s. Khamis was also passionate about broadcast media and became the first Emirati female TV host, working for Dubai Channel 2 in 1973.[21] Hessa Al Ossaily, like Khamis, was passionate about broadcast media and had the opportunity to study Arabic literature at one of Egypt's leading universities, Ain Shams. In 1965, she became the first Emirati female radio host to work for Dubai's Sout Al Sahel (Voice of the seacoast) radio station. By the mid-1970s, she was working as a host for Kuwait Television, which had an office in Dubai. Later, she moved to Abu Dhabi Television, where she became the first Emirati woman to serve as broadcasting director.[22]

J.M. has been working in the industry for more than ten years. She received a bachelor's degree in media and public relations from Ajman University in the mid-1980s and has been recognised for her exclusive news features, which have included interviews with the former ruler of Ras Al Khaimah[23] and the Crown Prince of Ajman.[24] Her illiterate mother inspired her to continue studying when she almost dropped out of high school. She said:

> I haven't faced societal restrictions…. My husband and children have been great supporters and understood the demands of my profession as a news correspondent, particularly the overseas travel. Even when I was a student, my husband took great pride in my academic achievement and encouraged me to attend evening classes at the university while he took care of the children's needs in my absence.

The expansion of the state education system and the development of the media infrastructure in the Emirates, including the launch of media hubs that host international press agencies in Abu Dhabi and Dubai, have offered the millennial generation of Emirati female journalists a better platform for bargaining with the patriarchs in regard to women's empowerment in the media. For example, in 2011, Hala Al Gergawi became the youngest ever Emirati executive managing editor and editor-in-chief of *Zahrat Al Khaleej* magazine, founded in 1979. Asserting that she has not encountered societal stereotypes or restrictions associated with her tribal background, she has established a legal publishing house and released three issues of a monthly bilingual magazine, *Tea Before Noon,* in which she published interviews with young business entrepreneurs. She said:

> I was the first female member to study abroad, to have her photographs published in newspapers and magazines, and to appear in televised interviews.

Shamsa Saif Al Hanaee, who became the first female and youngest sports reporter for *Al Ittihad*, was supported by her family, though she does feel that social norms limited her assertiveness at the start of her reporting career:

> My father is proud of me, and always reads my sports features. I was very shy and unsure of myself. It wasn't easy for me to meet with sources or even ask for a short statement. But with practise, I gained confidence, built a reputation for myself as a sports reporter, and established a strong relationship with sources in the sports field.

Likewise, Mona Al-Hmoudi, who delivers lectures to female undergraduate journalism majors, received family support and encouragement. 'In fact', she said:

> my eldest sister worked as a journalist for *Al Bayan* newspaper before [becoming] an executive director for the communications department at the Federal National Council. My husband supports me immensely. He is very proud of my accomplishments as a journalist and ... would even join me in the field to help with interviewing members of the public and gather data for my news features. He understands the demands of my job, especially when I am required to travel abroad. I recently travelled to Russia and Malaysia to cover governmental initiatives, and left him alone with our two-year-old son.

In the case of Badria Al Kassar, her father inspired her to pursue a career in journalism. In 1999, she did her internship at *Al Khaleej* newspaper, a Sharjah daily, where she published numerous environmental features about sea pollution. She subsequently worked for *Al Ittihad*'s office in the emirate of Fujairah and later moved to Abu Dhabi to work at the newspaper's headquarters. She recalled:

> My father was an illiterate. He worked as a shipmaster and a pearl diver. He raised me up with an open mind. He taught me how to be autonomous, how to make decisions, and granted me freedom of expression inside and outside the realm of our home. He never disapproved of my choice of journalism as an academic major, to the extent that he would invite my classmates to assist them with their media writing projects in which he would relate tales about the sea and astrology, about which he was an expert.
>
> All in all, my family supported me and understood the demands of my career, especially the domestic travel and the overseas tours.... My last overseas tour was to Jordan, where I visited the UAE's refugee camps at Mrajeeb Al Fhood area to report on the UAE Red Crescent's humanitarian efforts.

Resisting the patriarchal system

All of these testimonials reveal one side of the story: Emirati female journalists live in a society that glorifies the concept of tribal belonging and abide by a complex kinship system in which they must protect their honour and chastity in both private and public to maintain tribal purity, or *asil*, reputation, and honour. Their situation mirrors that of women in Saudi society, as memorably described by Pierre Bourdieu, in which 'a woman's foremost duty to self and family is to safeguard herself against all critical allusions to her sexual modesty: in dress, looks, attitudes, and speech, as shame reflects directly on parents and brothers'.[25] However, when I interviewed Arab expat female journalists working in the Emirates, I realised that they have been forced to carry the burden of societal restrictions too, if differently: they have been exposed to the patriarchal system's ideology of misogyny.

One Arab expat journalist, Lahib Abdulkhaliq, expressed the view that tribal patriarchalism is dominant in her country, Iraq, which shares borders with the Arab Gulf states of Saudi Arabia and Kuwait. This cultural heritage has affected her position in the media despite her journalistic accomplishments, which date back to 1979:

> I was the only Iraqi female war correspondent at that time. I covered the Second Battle of Al Faw[26] and the Halabja[27] chemical attack. My family disapproved of my work in the field of journalism, and would often mock me for working in a profession that they described as rubbish, just because I come from a prominent Iraqi tribe.... Today, I give lectures to undergraduate students majoring in journalism. I often encourage them by stressing the fact that our generation has paved the way for them to be seen and to be heard.

Regarding the misogynistic ideology of patriarchy, Najat Fares Al Fares, a Jordanian journalist for *Al Khaleej* newspaper who has written more than 200 features and won the Arab Journalism Award for outstanding investigative journalism, recalled her brothers' reaction after she received her degree from Al Quds University in Palestine: 'When my father printed a congratulatory note in a local newspaper in Palestine after my graduation, my brothers argued with him for printing the words "my daughter, the journalist". They didn't want me to work in this profession'.

In contrast, a small group of Arab expat female journalists said in their interviews that they did not encounter objections from their families in regards to studying and working in journalism, nor did they feel subjected to societal constraints. Hala Al Khayyat, a Jordanian journalist for *Al Ittihad*, described how her father, though illiterate, 'pushed me to study and work as a journalist, and never objected to my decision when I accepted this job offer and moved to the Emirates, against the wishes of my brothers though. My husband understands the demands of my job because he is a journalist too'.

Like Hala, Jalila, a Jordanian editor at *Al Ittihad* who worked as a reporter for *Al Hayat* newspaper in London and conducted an exclusive interview with former UN Secretary General Kofi Annan, attributes her success to her father. He 'inspires me', she said:

> He has a moderate opinion of Islam as a religion, and believes in the necessity of women's empowerment. He has never interfered in my decisions,

which may be judged negatively and stereotypically by people within Arab conservative societies. When I changed my academic major from dentistry to journalism, he supported me and continued to do so when I decided to marry a foreigner and move to live in the Emirates.

Laila Hafez, an Egyptian journalist who has been working for *Zahrat Al Khaleej* magazine for 30 years, started her career in Egypt soon after graduating from Cairo University in 1980. She said, 'From a family perspective, I have not met any challenge. You see, my husband is also a journalist; we graduated from the same university…. My husband supports me at every level'.

Alaa Abed Al Ghani, a Syrian journalist for *Al Khaleej*, feels she has been blessed by having a family system that provides her with practical and emotional support. She proudly said:

> Working in *Al Khaleej* was a dream come true. Since I was a little girl, I witnessed my beloved grandfather reading this newspaper from front to back cover…. After accepting the job offer, I broke the happy news to him first. He was very proud of the fact that his granddaughter would work for his favourite newspaper.
>
> Of course, my husband reads everything that I write. He even posts all my features in his Facebook account. He motivated me to complete my under-graduate studies at the college of communication in the University of Damascus, even though I struggled to finish my senior year and submit the capstone project in Beirut because of the civil war in Syria…. He always motivates me by saying, 'Invest in your talent. I have faith in you'.

Muna Saeed Al Taher, an Iraqi field reporter for *Al Roeya* newspaper, was the only interviewee who described facing familial disapproval due to reasons other than the stereotypes that surround the media industry. The source of her family's disapproval, rather, was their country's political environment, as the regime of dictator Saddam Hussein regularly imprisoned and executed journalists.

Whatever their specific level of familial support, it appears that female journalists in the Emirates are as yet unable to break the chains of patriarchy and its ideologies, whether based on kin ties, tribal class, or misogyny, that pressure and oppress them because no independent civil society is permitted to develop in the UAE. Efforts to transform the current social system and challenge the patriarchs to accept social change are solely driven by the neotraditional leadership of the UAE, which seeks to narrow the gender gap through orchestrated state emancipation campaigns to sustain its political authority and international image as a modern state. This is discussed at length in the next and final findings chapter, which focuses on the state's contradictory role in empowering women while still holding them accountable for preserving traditions and subordinating their position within the family by reinforcing family laws.

Conclusion

Using empirical evidence from participant observation and in-depth interviews, this chapter has examined the impact of tribal patriarchalism and tribal belonging on female journalists in the Emirates. With society proving to be resistant to change and apprehensive of the state's top-down strategies, tribal patriarchalism and belonging have put limitations on the development of a concrete women's journalism movement in the Emirates, as well as restrictions on their right of choice and expression, particularly voicing their investment in expanding gender equality and women's social and legal rights.

This chapter has also explored how the divide between Emirati women of different social classes has widened, with opportunities for empowerment made available almost exclusively to women who belong to the elite tribe class. The fact is that these women act as symbols for the state, which empowers them to receive mainly international recognition instead of acting as game changers to transform women's status in the Emirates. Meanwhile, intellectual middle-class women are sidelined and largely absent from decision-making positions and public life in general, depriving them of the opportunity to lobby the political powers for social and civil change in the Emirates, which should start with amending the current family law to better respect women's rights.

In sum, the concept of 'equal citizen' does not exist in the UAE because of tribal stratification, the paltry 'gender balance' strategies developed by the government to address women's rights and challenge the existing gendered social practices, the lack of freedom of opinion and political diversity, and the nonexistence of feminist movements due to the deficient self-awareness of women in the Emirates.

Notes

1 Ismail (2011).
2 Moghadam (2003, p. 113).
3 Maisel (2014, p. 102).
4 Ibid., p. 103.
5 Moghadam (2003, p. 143).
6 Maisel (2014, p. 103).
7 Garcia (2023).
8 Heard-Bey (2005, p. 361).
9 Young (2016, p. 12).
10 Founded by Imam Malek ibn Anas (d. 759 CE), who led the traditionalist movement in Mecca and Medina, 'the Maleki school advocates the notion of the Medina consensus as the only authoritative form of consensus and source of law achieved by relying heavily on prophetic hadiths' (Cornell, 2007, p. 160).
11 Moghadam (2003, p. 122).
12 Maisel (2014, p. 118).
13 Ibid.
14 The first elections for the FNC were held in December 2006. The term of office is four years.
15 Salem (2015).
16 Özev (2017, p. 1013).

17 Before the discovery of oil, during the last British Expedition in 1819, Emirati males and females received only modest education from Najdian scholars, who held classes in mosques. They taught mathematics, Quranic studies, and Arabic grammar. The first school and public library, Al Taymiyah, was established in Sharjah in 1907 (Hassan, 2011, p. 124).
18 Al Breiki is one of the prominent Emirati tribes.
19 A popular Emirati presenter who hosts a poetry contest show, *Al Shara* (Insignia).
20 Simonson and Park (2016, p. 485).
21 Salih (1983).
22 Hassan (2011).
23 Sheikh Saqr bin Mohammad Al Qassimi (1920–2010) was the ruler of Ras Al Khaimah, a northern emirate bordering Oman's exclave of Musandam.
24 Sheikh Rashid bin Humaid Al Nuaimi (1984–present) is the Crown Prince of Ajman, the smallest in area of the seven federal emirates.
25 Cited in Moghadam (2003, p. 119).
26 Fought on 17 April 1988, this was a major battle of the Iran–Iraq war, in which the Iraqi Army, led by Saddam Hussein, conducted a 36-hour operation to clear the Iranians out of the Al Faw peninsula after a two-year occupation.
27 A massacre against the Kurdish people that took place on 16 March 1988, during the closing days of the Iran–Iraq war in the city of Halabja in Southern Kurdistan.

References

Cornell, V. (2007). *Voices of Islam*. Westport, CT: Praeger Publishers.
Garcia, A. (2023). 'Emiratization in the UAE Explained'. *Economy Middle East*. Available at: https://economymiddleeast.com/news/emiratization-in-the-uae-explained/ [Accessed 21 February 2020].
Hassan, A. (2011). *Our Media Identity*. Dubai: Fujairah Media and Culture Authority.
Heard-Bey, F. (2005). *From Trucial States to United Arab Emirates*. London: Motivate.
Ismail, M. (2011). 'Media Needs More Female Emirati Journalists'. *The National*. 28 March. Available at: http://www.thenational.ae/news/uae-news/media-needs-more-female-emirati-journalists [Accessed 14 June 2017].
Maisel, S. (2014). *The New Rise of Tribalism in Saudi Arabia*. London: White Horse Press.
Moghadam, V. (2003). *Modernizing Women: Gender and Social Change in the Middle East*. Boulder, CO: L. Rienner.
Özev, M. (2017). 'Saudi Society and the State: Ideational and Material Basis'. *Arab Studies Quarterly*, 39(4), p. 1013.
Salem, O. (2015). 'UAE People & Politics: One Person, One Vote to Shake Up This Year's FNC Election'. *The National*. 25 June. Available at: https://www.thenational.ae/uae/government/uae-people-politics-one-person-one-vote-to-shake-up-this-year-s-fnc-election-1.104827 [Accessed 9 June 2020].
Salih, L. (1983). *Women's Literature in the Arab Gulf*. Translated by the author. Kuwait: Dar Al Yaqatha Publications.
Simonson, P. and Park, D. (2016). *International History of Communication Study*. New York, NY: Routledge.
Young, K. (2016). *Women's Labor Force Participation Across the GCC*. Washington, DC: Arab Gulf States Institute in Washington.

8 State Feminism

Empowerment, Gender Balance, and Nation-Branding

For the past three decades, the neo-traditionalist leadership of the Emirates has been using women's empowerment as one of its key instruments in nation-building and -branding. As scholar Melissa Aronczyk has described, 'nation-branding is a particular version of national identity that allows national governments to better manage and control the image they project to the world'.[1] Implemented in every institution to raise the Emirati people's sense of national loyalty, pride, and security, the leadership has made sure that nation-branding, whatever contemporary elements it embraces, does not deviate from the core components of the state's continued existence: tradition and religion.

Cultural anxiety over the erosion of religious authenticity and the obscuration of the Emirates' unique history and heritage has led to conflicting understandings of empowerment and how (or even if) to reinforce it in the national economic and legal spheres. In a 2005 study, scholars Ruth Alsop and Nina Heinson examined the domains and measurements of empowerment in four countries to identify the roles of the state, in which a person is a civic actor; the role of the market, in which a person is an economic actor; and the role of the society, in which a person is a social actor.[2] After applying the Measuring Empowerment (ME) framework in Ethiopia, Nepal, Honduras, and Mexico,[3] they concluded that for women to be empowered, they need to 'understand their own self-worth, to have the right to own and/or have access to resources and opportunities, and to enjoy the freedom to make decisions about issues in all aspects of life that pertain/affect them'.[4]

For Emirati women, achieving those benchmarks is difficult to contemplate because of deep-rooted familial, social, religious, and cultural restraints. Opportunities for them to progress are limited since tribal patriarchy and the law restrict their freedom, will, and choice as individuals. For instance, married women must obtain their guardian's (husband's) approval before starting a career, while single women must obtain their guardian's (father's, paternal uncle's, or eldest brother's) consent to conclude their marriage contracts. Such controls on women's rights have resulted in increasing the ratio of unemployed women to unemployed men in the Emirates to ten to one. Their financial autonomy is likewise impeded: while 90 percent of Emirati men hold bank accounts, only 60 percent of Emirati women do.[5]

DOI: 10.4324/9781003488415-8

Within this framework, this final finding chapter examines the historical progression of Emirati women's societal role before their integration into the Emirati state's nation-building scheme. It addresses the anomalies that arise with the Emirati state's approach to empowering Emirati women while holding on to convention in the face of rapid social change and deeming them to be the carriers of the so-called traditions that those in power select and reinvent according to their own purposes. Though state-backed empowerment campaigns for education and the employment of Emirati women were launched soon after the country's 1971 federal union, they have still not been fully accepted by the resilient tribal patriarchal society.

Assessing Emirati women's condition before 1971

During the nineteenth and early 20th centuries, women in the Trucial States established a strong matriarchal system. They were in absolute control of family affairs, debt payments, investments, and business affairs at the marketplace, especially during the pearl diving season that extended from June to October. As both breadwinners and child bearers, women ensured the tribe's survival since men were absent for long periods of time, risking their lives in the ocean. The hardship of tribal life in the desert made sexual segregation and ancient conventional values difficult to maintain, and men were dependent in many ways on women. The need for women's presence in commercial affairs was even raised by men, who, in response to an incident in Dubai's fish market in 1931, protested the Legislative Council's decision forbidding women from selling fish alongside men. Local men argued that they spent most of their day in the boat fishing, while women were adept at selling the daily catch at the best prices due to their persuasive techniques and understanding of the market.[6]

Trucial women also practised different professions without restriction,[7] ranging from tutoring to midwifery and medicine, challenging the modern medical techniques of the American missionary doctors who arrived in the region in 1909 with traditional medicine based on remedies used by the Prophet and the ancient Greeks.[8] One of the most prominent women physicians was Hamama Obaid Al Tunaiji, who during the 1940s and 1950s treated men, women, and children for various physical and psychological diseases, such as asthma, nephritic syndrome, and paranoia, with herbal treatments that she devised out of fennel flower seeds and turmeric, or traditional remedies that she learned from her aunt, who practised midwifery.[9]

Nonetheless, Trucial women's social conditions and their health remained problematic, due to the continuing practice of tribal traditions, which women also encouraged, such as child marriage and the exclusive use of herbal treatments to treat women, who often had no access to modern medicine. In her missionary reports, American physician Marian Kennedy wrote that child marriages were a social norm, and a girl of seven, eight, or nine would be married to an older man with the aim of producing large numbers of children (preferably male heirs) from an early age. This, she said, resulted in the deterioration of these young girls' health and death at an early age in childbirth due to the deficient medical treatments that they received from local midwives, who often used rock salt as a contraceptive.[10]

While polygamy, a sign of wealth, was widespread amongst the ruling class and merchant families, Trucial women had to endure the act of divorce in a largely illiterate society that lacked legislation to protect divorcees. As a consequence, divorced women in the Trucial States were forced to struggle alone for survival. In an anthropological study documenting Emirati women's pre-oil history, author Nick Forster interviewed a 75-year-old grandmother in 2010, who said that after her divorce, 'I had no choice but to open a small shop to provide a living for my five sons. I sold fish and clothes. In the beginning of my journey in business, I faced many difficulties, like rumours about breaking our culture norms. But soon, other women began to open their own shops and businesses'.[11]

The Trucial States' economic growth remained modest, and women's low socio-economic status persisted throughout the 1930s, a period that witnessed enormous oil excavation campaigns in the area led by Iraq Petroleum Company's representative, William Richard Williamson. Known to the local people as *Haji* Williamson, he was given a two-year licence to excavate oil in Abu Dhabi for 3,000 rupees (£27,000 in today's money) on 5 January 1936. Subsequently, other Western companies arrived in the area for oil excavation, such as British Petroleum and the French Petroleum Company (Total). The discovery of oil was made official years later, in 1958, when French excavator Jacques Cousteau and his research team onboard the vessel *Calypso* drilled under the sea at a depth of 8,755 feet. However, oil revenue was not put to use for national development until December 1963, when the first oil tanker left Jebel Al Dhanna Port in Abu Dhabi.[12]

From the 1930s to the mid-1960s, the newfound oil wealth brought gradual advancements to Trucial society, particularly affecting women, who were exposed to rising Arab liberation and feminist movements, as well as to Arab literature through the modest availability of printed publications and the establishment of schools across the region. This began with Sharjah's Al Qassemia School in 1953, followed in 1964 by six schools in Abu Dhabi, funded by early oil revenues, where 528 students, including 138 female students, were enrolled.[13] Britain also contributed to the education of the Trucial people during the colonial period by establishing a number of technical schools which offered courses in carpentry, vehicle maintenance, electrical installation, mechanical engineering, and agriculture in the emirate of Sharjah in 1958, the emirate of Dubai in 1964, and the emirate of Ras Al Khaimah in 1969.[14] The modest output of the printing press also contributed to an evolution in the mindset of Trucial youth, who launched newspapers to criticise British interventions in local matters and call for independence, such as *Sout Al Asafeer* (Birds tweet), which was launched in 1933 by a group of young people from Dubai and Sharjah.[15]

In his memoir *The Arab of the Desert*, Lieutenant Colonel H. R. P. Dickson wrote about how print and broadcast media altered public views of British colonisation:

> In 1956, people started to listen to the radio broadcast news, which was largely aired by Egypt's radio station Sawt Al Arab [Voice of the Arabs],

aiming to receive updates on the major events taking place in the Middle East, particularly the 1948 Arab-Israeli conflict in Palestine. People also began to read the analytical news reports that were published in regional Arabic and Indian newspapers.[16] The change of views affected our presence in the area and altered our relationship disappointingly with the Arabs in neighboring states.[17]

By the early 1960s, journalism had become a platform for the youth to express their views and share their political struggle against colonialism with others in the Arab region. For example, Salem Ali Al Owais wrote columns for *Al Shura* (Consultation) newspaper and his brother Ahmad for *Al Risalah* (Message), while Ahmad bin Sultan wrote columns for *Al Shabab* (Youth), all of which were printed in Egypt. Ahmad Amin Al Madani wrote columns for several newspapers, including *Al Adab* (Literature), which was printed in Beirut, and *Al Qabas* (Firebrand) and *Al Zaman* (Times), which were printed in Baghdad.[18]

This youth cultural movement and its contribution to literature disclose a hidden history of artistic innovation by the young men and women of the Trucial States, which took the forms of colloquial or Nabatean poetry, folk storytelling, and acting. Leading figures include the poets Mubarak Al Nakhi (1900–1982) and Salem bin Ali Al Owais (1887–1959); the novelists Shaikha Al Nakhi, author of *Qisat Al Raheel* (*Story of departure*), and Abdulla Saqr, who wrote *Qoloub La Tarham* (*Merciless hearts*) in the early 1960s; and the actor Ali Bu Ruhaima, the first Emirati to perform on stage at Al Qassemia School's theatre during the 1950s.[19]

Oil wealth, the Emirati state, and the integration of women

The increase of oil wealth, followed by political independence and the formation of the United Arab Emirates in December 1971 as a rentier state, comprising seven federal emirates, marked an evolutionary transition for Trucial society, women in particular, whose empowerment and emancipation became an integral part of the state's nation-building project. With the support of the nation's founding father, the late Sheikh Zayed Bin Sultan Al Nahyan, and the ruling families,[20] women gained access to education and employment and were closely involved in the national economic development plan. To convince the tribal society of the importance of women's emancipation to the development of the nation's economy, the newly born state and its neo-traditionalist leadership gradually refashioned the traditional values of the society through the establishment of various women's empowerment campaigns and organisations under the patronage of the rulers' wives. The aim was to reshape the conservative teachings of Islam that society had long observed by promoting Islamic feminism—a patriarchal vision to control women's participation, casting them as social negotiators rather than decision-makers.[21]

Women's literacy and education became a central pillar in the nation-building project. In the 1970s, the state opened and funded 350 schools, in which 94,425 students were enrolled and 7,849 teachers were registered.[22] The state census report published in 1975 revealed that 3,005 female students received undergraduate university degrees and made-up 46 percent of the inaugural class at the UAE University in 1976, and more than 65 percent in the 1980s. By 1995, the number of female students registered at the state's first university had reached 61,496. Women's literacy levels continued to rise by the decade, from 37.7 percent in 1970 to 59 percent in 1980, 70.6 percent in 1990, and 79.1 percent in 2000.[23]

With undergraduate and postgraduate university degrees in hand, literate women were able to join the labour force and contribute to the development of the national economy and security. In 1977, the Ministry of Education employed 2,375 female teachers, of whom 199 (8.4 percent) were Emiratis, as well as 551 female administrators, of whom 128 (23 percent) were Emiratis. In addition, in 1977, the Ministry of Interior hired Emirati women in the police unit as inspectors. In Abu Dhabi, 24 female Emirati inspectors joined the police unit, while 18 female Emirati inspectors joined the police unit in Dubai.[24]

Nevertheless, women's education and employment were restricted because some academic degrees and professions were viewed as off-limits to them, particularly journalism. The launch of several government-owned and private newspapers, as well as the inauguration of the Ministry of Information and Culture in 1975, the Emirates News Agency (WAM) in 1976,[25] and the first academic journalism programme at the UAE University in 1977, reflected the state's modernisation agenda, crucial to which was building a strong foundation for its media industry. Employment opportunities were created, legislation was passed, and up-to-date technologies were applied to the production of print and broadcast media—all under the rubric of patriotism. This has influenced Emirati women journalists' outlook on their state-backed empowerment and emancipation, especially in the media industry, which gradually came to be seen as no longer off limits, as detailed in the following observations and testimonials.

Reflecting on her role in the state-backed empowerment campaign for Emirati female journalists, Fatema Al Senani, who describes herself as *Bent Al Balad* (daughter of the nation), stated:

> I promote our national identity through filming projects that address patriotic causes, aiming to instil our unique heritage and legacy in the younger generation of Emiratis, and to honour our family values. Executives within government and semi-government authorities support Emirati women's emancipation project by policy making and in practise. For instance, when I enter the royal court[26] as a camerawoman to film an official event or a reception, I often stand in a special location, allocated just for me. From there I can conveniently capture exclusive moments through my lens and conduct one-on-one interviews with male members of the royal family.

Likewise, F.H. strongly believes in the impact of her role in showcasing the state's support for Emirati women, who are 'empowered more than men', as she put it. She said:

> Through my live talk show, I aim to change society's stereotypical views on women's rights. I aim for the world to witness the real image of Emirati women: they are not oppressed, their career choices are not limited, and they are empowered more than men, both economically and politically. Today, we owe it to the state that Emirati women have become ministers and judges. In my talk show, I interview Emirati female doctors and surgeons who specialize in complicated medical fields.

Emirati female journalists are using the media as a platform to confirm their presence and emphasise the Emirati state's backing for their emancipation and participation in the nation's political and economic development. J.M. said:

> Today, Emirati women receive an endless amount of support from the government's leadership to secure their empowerment in a gender equal society. In this sense, Emirati women's empowerment is evident in my workplace, where my male line manager ensures that my career development is guaranteed. The UAE labour law grants Emirati women rights, including *equal* pay and full pay when on maternity leave.

Mahra Al Jenaibi praised the UAE leadership for encouraging Emirati female journalists and promoting their journalistic work. She said:

> I once went out into the field with a cameraman to do a report on a local exhibition. There, I tried to get hold of Sheikh Nahyan bin Mubarak Al Nahyan[27] to get an exclusive statement, but I was crammed between a dozen male reporters. He saw the situation I was in and asked all the male reporters to give me some space, and started talking to me first before giving the rest any further statements. I also did a news report on the first Emirati female crane operator, who was working for Zayed Port. When the report was uploaded in our official Twitter account, Sheikh Abdulla bin Zayed Al Nahyan[28] retweeted it.

Al Jenaibi's testimonial speaks to the fact that Emirati women working for the broadcast media in the Emirates do not feel disempowered. I observed this closely at the Dubai and Abu Dhabi newsrooms, despite the lack of access to internal corporate statistics that could have supported my argument about the glass ceiling effect in Emirati newsrooms. In the Dubai newsroom, additionally, I observed the professional competition between Emirati female and male journalists, where some humorously labelled the newsroom community as 'the feminine society' because the civil labour law and internal corporate internal policies granted women more benefits than men, such as full pay when on leave.

In fact, UAE labour law safeguards Emirati women's employment and economic rights. In 2019, an amendment to the law was set forth by the UAE's president, Sheikh Khalifa Bin Zayed Al Nahyan, to ensure equal access to opportunities for Emirati women and that they are not subjected to discrimination and danger in the workplace. One article in the amended law states that 'an employer may not discriminate against an employee based on her pregnancy'.[29] In addition, articles 29 and 32 state that 'no women shall be employed on any job that is hazardous, arduous or physically or morally detrimental' and that 'a female wage shall be equal to that of a male if she performs the same work'.[30]

I observed how the producers and directors of Dubai's *Akhbar Al Emarat* and Abu Dhabi's *Oloum Al Dar* news broadcasts represent Emirati women to demonstrate their vital role in national development. They would often invite successful Emirati women to appear on air as guests or conduct short phone interviews to address national issues. Her Excellency Dr. Rauda Al Saadi, Director General of the Executive Committee Office in Abu Dhabi, appeared on set, on day three of my observations on site in the Abu Dhabi newsroom, to talk about a new government initiative: a law to promote the reading of Arabic literature to preserve the language. In another news broadcast, which aired on 14 February 2017, an Emirati executive guest was received at the *Akhbar Al Emarat* studio to talk about Dubai's latest initiative, the Hackathon of Happiness. Her Excellency Dr. Aisha Bin Bishr, Director General of the Smart Dubai Office, talked about Happiness Hack Dubai: The Smart Travel Experience, launched to market Dubai as the happiest city in the world.

From this perspective, the neo-traditionalist leadership of the Emirates has been investing in Emirati women's education, recognising them as equal partners in national development, and continuing to pursue a strategy of empowering women in cultural, social, and economic fields. In the 2023 Global Gender Gap Report by the World Economic Forum, for instance, the Emirates secured the 35th position worldwide and topped the list regionally for its notable performance in the 'Political Empowerment' sub-index. Additionally, it was recognized as the MENA region's most equitable nation and ranked 22nd globally in the 2021–2022 Georgetown University WPS Index, focusing on women's inclusion, security, and access to justice. The advancement of Emirati women in both economic and political spheres has been closely linked to a notable surge in women's education. Presently, an impressive 95.8 percent of Emirati women have received formal education, with women constituting 70 percent of university graduates. Notably, 56 percent of these graduates specialize in science, mathematics, and engineering disciplines. The cabinet presently includes 9 female ministers among its 32 members, marking a significant stride towards gender parity. Moreover, in 2015, Dr. Amal Al Qubaisi made history as the first woman elected as Speaker of the Federal National Council (FNC), the UAE's parliamentary body, a position she first attained in 2006 as the pioneering woman to join the FNC.

From another perspective, Emirati male journalists interviewed for this study agreed that state efforts have improved the status of Emirati women over the years. For example, Mohamed Al Hammadi said, 'In the Emirates, we don't have an issue against women because we believe in their vital role as partners in the national development'. Emirati male journalists not only praised the state for empowering women but also recognised the importance of their journalistic work in supporting the nation-building process. Abdulla Abdulkarim stated:

Through my work as a journalist, I have come to the realization that I am carrying a heavy burden: supporting my nation's development and addressing the Emirati peoples' causes.... Gender inequality does not exist in the media industry or in any other industry in the Emirates. Emirati women are fully endorsed, even here at this corporation, and we, as men, are jealous of that!

Arab expat journalists also expressed their admiration for the Emirates' leadership and its efforts to ensure the advancement of Emirati women, especially in the field of media. For example, Rasha Tubeileh said, 'I have been living in the Emirates for the past ten years now. Times have changed and Emirati women's presence in this field has increased, erasing the negative stereotype about journalism as a disrespectful profession for women'. Reda El Bawardy goes even further:

The governing leadership and executives at major local media corporations work hand in hand to achieve the nation-building project's number one goal that aims towards empowering Emirati women and raising the glass ceiling in the workplace. I think that women are granted with windows of opportunities—they are empowered more than men here!

Alsayed Salama has a similar view of Emirati women's status:

I believe that Emirati women are appreciated and receive their rights fully. The Emirati state has developed an extraordinary plan to empower Emirati women by providing them with the topmost academic opportunities, and by ensuring their emancipation in the workplace, whilst keeping in mind protecting their privacy and needs through civil law and policy making.

Laila Hafez asserts that the Gulf States have created 'an ideal environment' for women:

Emirati women are seizing every opportunity granted to them on a plate of gold, owing to the president and his wife's determination towards achieving their empowerment. They are taking the lead as ministers and hold powerful positions. Because of the political and economic development, I think that Arab Gulf and Emirati women generally live in an ideal environment that allows for their growth and empowerment in comparison to Arab women nowadays, who are being oppressed and are literally moving backwards to the dark ages!

From a different angle, Alaa Abed Al Ghani noticed how the leadership pays attention to local news stories that can be leveraged to foster Emirati women's empowerment. She said:

Once, I conducted an interview with a very smart Emirati female undergraduate, who developed a scientific capstone project about the possibilities of establishing a space station on planet Mars. Officials at the UAE Space Agency called me soon after the news feature was published in the newspaper asking for the Emirati female undergraduate's contact details. They adopted her innovative scientific project and offered her a job opportunity. Officials tell me all the time that my work as a journalist complements their national duty towards the empowerment of Emirati women.

Likewise, Salam Abu Shihab strongly believes that journalism mirrors the Emirati state's nation-building scheme. The leadership is determined to empower both women and men to challenge outdated norms. He stated:

There is little to complain about in this society, you know why? Because the Emirati government is always one step ahead of the media. The government takes exceptional care of the Emirati people's well-being and has solved almost every problem that can cross your mind. For instance, the government has established the Marriage Fund to support Emirati newlyweds financially and provide them with a housing scheme too. The government has also developed a national scheme known as Emiratisation to ensure that Emiratis are employed in every sector, where they receive adequate career planning with training programmes, and are granted high wages and benefits. What else can we look for or be critical of when everything is secured and well provided?

Nonetheless, a small group of Emirati female journalists interviewed for this study affirmed to me that they feel disempowered because executives at media corporations challenge the Emirati state's investment in women's empowerment by fostering negative gender politics, which I observed inside the newsrooms in Abu Dhabi and Dubai. Media executives routinely offer work opportunities, promotions, and benefits unequally between male and female journalists. Yaqoutah Abdulla Al Dhanhane spoke of her experience at *Al Bayan* newspaper, where discrimination was evident and executives favoured Arab expat journalists over Emiratis, whom they viewed as threats to their career prospects—an ongoing conflict that impacts employment in the Emirates generally. She said:

The management feels apprehensive about the idea of empowering Emirati journalists and allowing them to hold senior positions within the corporation. Most of the Emiratis at that newspaper resigned due to the negative atmosphere in the workplace and the constant battle against us by the Arab expat journalists, who were scared of giving leadership positions to Emiratis! I know many classmates who majored in mass media and journalism and are still unemployed because they never had any opportunities.

But she also spoke highly of the state's support for journalism and, specifically, Emirati female journalists:

The ruler of Dubai launched the Dubai Future Accelerators initiative in 2016 to empower a new generation of Emirati media professionals. The launch came after an official visit that he made to the newspaper's head-quarters. He was very disappointed when he found out that there were only two Emirati journalists working for the newspaper. After the launch of this initiative, thousands of young Emirati journalists enrolled in the first cohort.... Soon afterwards, backed by the support of Dubai's ruler, Muna Busamra was appointed the editor-in-chief for *Al Bayan*, becoming the first Emirati female journalist to hold such a position in the history of Emirati journalism.

Not only gender politics but the fixed gender views in the UAE have also con-tributed to the gendered media atmosphere—Emirati and Arab expat men assess women's professional performances based on social and religious morality, which women submit to and which impacts negatively on their sense of self-worth and belief in their potential to excel professionally. While observing the newsroom ac-tivities in Dubai for two weeks, where the entire national news team was Emirati, I noticed that there were very few female field reporters compared to the number of Emirati male field reporters. Explaining this imbalance, one male senior editor said: 'Because of their nature and out of fear for their safety, we tend not to send females to cover news of accidents, let alone fires or wars'.

Leila addressed Emirati women's disempowerment by sociocultural factors while emphasising the importance of education in driving social change:

Yes, the glass ceiling is high, but it's not just only in journalism. I think it's across the board. I think one day we will get there. You have to re-member this is a very young nation. Definitely, the role of education is a huge one—we are not only educating the children, but also educating their parents because parents raise these children. So, I think education starts from the household, the mother, the father, their mentality, how they teach right from wrong to their children, teach them equality between brother and sister, teaching religion in a balanced way and not in an extreme form, that sort of thing.

Women should be strong and very confident no matter what they face; they should feel confident in their abilities and be open to growth and on developing themselves. I'm very big on supporting women, and so I feel women should always support each other. We should always champion each other, help each other through any adversity.

Leila's testimony suggests that Emirati women, especially middle-class educators, journalists, writers, intellectuals, and employees of government and semi-government entities, can transform society through political movement and activism. They can have an impact similar to that of their female counterparts in Arab states, such as Palestinian activist Hanan Ashrawi and Egyptian feminist Nawal El Saadawi.[31]

The UAE has its own examples of outstanding women capable of leading the discourse for social change. These include Sheikha Lubna Al Qassimi, who became the first woman to hold a ministerial post in the Emirates; Dr. Hessa Abdullah Lootah, who is known locally as the first lady of mass communication for her academic work, teaching journalism in the Emirates during the 1980s; writer Dhabiya Khamis; and Captain Aysha Al Hameli, who became the first Emirati woman to represent the UAE in the International Civil Aviation Organization (ICAO).

The collective work of educated women more generally is vital to the continued growth of female empowerment, legal rights, and social justice, as Moroccan feminist Fatima Mernissi has argued: 'It's these women, the teachers and others belonging to the petite bourgeoisie, who are in the process of changing the world around them, because their situation as it is, is untenable. There are too many archaic aspects in marriage, in the relations between the sexes, in the work situation. These educated women were nourished with a desire for independence'.[32]

Nevertheless, as explained in Chapter 7, tribal patriarchalism persists in the Emirates due to the distinctive social structure characterised by stratification by tribal class, which affects Emirati women's status and rights in family law. In the political realm, the neo-traditionalist leadership of the Emirates has integrated women into its nation-building scheme cautiously, that is, without upsetting the core of the Emirati social structure. In 1988, Turkish author Deniz Kandiyoti described this as the patriarchal gender contract, which 'is realized within the family and codified by the state.... States that legitimize their own power on patriarchal structures such as the extended family foster its perpetuation through legislation that subordinates women to the control of men'.[33]

Amongst the basic rights that have been denied to Emirati women is marrying a foreign citizen (either Arab or non-Arab)[34] without obtaining prior approval from the state authorities. Emirati men can marry foreigners without prior approval. Their wives gain full citizenship rights after seven years of marriage (according to Article 17/1972 of the law) and their children at birth.[35] Emirati women's foreign husbands are not given Emirati citizenship. As for their children, they likewise do not become Emirati citizens, taking only their father's citizenship until the age of 18. Only then can they request to be granted Emirati citizenship by the civil court, which is entirely at the court's discretion.

It is apparent that state-backed empowerment opportunities and attempts to achieve gender balance are less than successful because of the unconscious gender biases that Emirati men and women hold and the belief that men and women cannot be equal because they are not identical physically or psychologically. As psychologist Virginia Valian has explained, 'The most important consequence of this for professional work is that men are consistently overrated, while women are underrated. Thus, professional women are at a slight disadvantage in every interaction, and these disadvantages accumulate over time to be big differences'.[36]

In the UAE constitution, the issue of women's equality is not explicitly addressed. Women's social, economic, and legal rights are not fully acknowledged due to the traditional religious and patriarchal biases that constrain and isolate them, putting them at the mercy of their male relatives, who act as their guardians and have the legal authority to prevent them from participating in the workforce. As a result, there are no national or international organisations that promote gender equality in the UAE, except for the state-backed UAE Women's Association, which is operated under the patronage of Shaikha Fatima bint Mubarak, wife of the late Sheikh Zayed Bin Sultan Al Nahyan.[37] And in turn, the UAE Women's Association works to foster conservative notions of women's maternal role and the values of family. Advocates of the social structure based on tribal patriarchalism blame the rise of social problems, like drug addiction and domestic violence by abusive spouses, on the state's over-employment and empowerment of women. This explains the Emirati state's approach to maintaining the gender contract by maintaining public patriarchy.

Emirati women are thus subordinated within Islamic family law, and their empowerment within the state's nation-building scheme is shaped to ensure that they play the role of carriers of the so-called traditions. The ideology behind this approach mirrors in multiple ways that of US conservatism, as in Rebecca Klatch's description:

> The ideal society, then, is one in which individuals are integrated into a moral community, bound together by faith, by common moral values, and by obeying the dictates of the family and religion.... While male and female roles are each respected and essential and complementary components of God's plan, men are the spiritual leaders and decision-makers in the family. It is women's role to support men in their position of higher authority through altruism and self-sacrifice.[38]

Even though fathers, husbands, and other male relatives continue to exercise legal authority over women in various ways for reasons associated with religion and tradition, the country has made considerable changes to empower Emirati women, improve their lives, and integrate them into the workforce in multiple sectors, including the media. The World Economic Forum's Global Gender Gap 2021 report recognised the Emirates for increasing women's literacy levels and incomes. The UAE ranked first overall across the Arab world in the GGP report and first or tied for first globally in four of the report's indicators: women in parliament; sex ratio at birth; literacy rate; and enrolment in primary education.

Obedience to tribal traditions and past legacies reflects honour, or *sharaf*, as Emirati people express it. *Sharaf* influences people's behaviour and outlook on life, as is apparent even today in their genuine political loyalty to the authoritarian leadership, their commitment to preserving past tribal allegiances through intermarriages, and their obligation towards tribal reconciliation in cases of conflict, even with constitutional civil law.

Emirati men and women alike still obey these tribal traditions. But it is mostly women who carry the heavy burden of tribal honour, both in private—lacking freedom of choice in marriage, for instance, in which selecting a partner for the reason of love is still considered shameful—and in public—lacking freedom of expression and choice, again, in creating their own future as independent individuals. For example, a woman's decision to obtain a higher degree or a full-time career is still dealt with as a family matter, in which the guardian, in the form of a father, eldest brother, or husband, has the final say.

Increased access to education and employment has had a significant impact on three generations of Emirati women's consciousness regarding gender and their rights, as this study has examined, and on their desire to achieve autonomy and to implement a social discourse for the transformation of the patriarchal gender contract. The forces that continue to stand in the way of Emirati women include their own lack of confidence due to being confined psychologically by socio-culturally biased gender roles, limited access to full participation in the nation-building scheme, and the deficiency of state-backed campaigns in granting Emirati women equal family rights.

To tackle these issues, Emirati women need to comprehend the notion of citizenship because only then, as author Aziz Al Azmeh argued, can 'the struggle for citizenship ... complete the transition from communal to civil society'.[39] But this transition, like all historical processes, is highly conflictual due to the persistence of tribal patriarchalism in the case of the Emirates specifically and the Arab Gulf states generally. In the absence of activism and progressive social movements in the Emirates, it is Emirati women's fight against tribal patriarchalism that will bring about social change and eliminate discrimination. What Emirati journalist Ayesha Al Mazroui wrote a decade ago remains true today: 'The fact that we have made great progress in terms of narrowing the gender gap should not lead us into complacency, thinking that the required progress has been made and that no further efforts are necessary'.[40]

Conclusion

Using empirical evidence from participant observation and in-depth interviews, this chapter examined how the patriarchal contract has thwarted Emirati women from achieving full autonomy and equality, conflicting with articles 14 and 25 of the UAE constitution, which guarantee all persons' equality, social justice, and equal opportunity and affirm that they are equal before the law without distinction by race or social status.

Despite those constitutional promises, Emirati women's rights are not fully recognised by the state's empowerment strategies due to the dominance of tribal patriarchalism in society. Emirati women are particularly disadvantaged in the family law regarding marriage and marriage dissolution, in which they may lose custody over their children as a result of remarriage, for instance, confirming yet again that the nation-building scheme is shaped to ensure patriarchal control within the law, maintaining the state's political 'authenticity'.

These legal deficiencies stifle the prospects of Emirati women, who are viewed as social negotiators and protectors of traditions rather than autonomous decision-makers. In the media field specifically, as explored earlier, the current corporate laws reflect patriarchal gender views, reinforcing the glass ceiling and amplifying professional inequalities and discrimination. In sum, the current state strategies and corporate laws reinforce traditional roles for Emirati women rather than promoting anything close to true equality.

Notes

1 Lerner (1986, p. 217).
2 Stephens and Al Nahyan (2018).
3 Ibid.
4 Ekerstedt (2014, p. 4).
5 Ekerstedt (2014).
6 Sonbol (2012).
7 Excepting the sheikhs' wives and upper-class women, who were dependent on their husbands' wealth and were concerned with charity work. However, a few upper-class women contributed to the economy by using their personal wealth, which was often inherited, to establish pearl-trading businesses, such as Sheikha Hussa Bint Al Murr Bin Huraiz, mother of the former Ruler of Dubai Sheikh Rashid Bin Saeed Al Maktoum (1912–1990) (Sonbol, 2012, p. 164).
8 Sonbol (2012).
9 Salem (2014).
10 Sonbol (2012, p. 252).
11 Forster (2017, p. 40).
12 Moheisen (2015).
13 Foley (2010, p. 176).
14 Soffan (1980, p. 51).
15 Ezzat (1983).
16 Most of the rich merchants on the coastal side of the peninsula spoke Urdu fluently at the time due to their close economic ties with India.
17 Ezzat (1983, p. 50).
18 Nafadi (1996, p. 40).
19 Alrai (2010).
20 The seven federal emirates are ruled by six families: Al Nahyan in Abu Dhabi, Al Maktoum in Dubai, Al Qassimi in Sharjah and Ras Al Khaimah, Al Nuaimi in Ajman, Al Mualla in Umm Al Qaiwain, and Al Sharqi in Fujairah.
21 Sonbol (2012).
22 Soffan (1980, p. 51).
23 Foley (2010, p. 182).
24 Soffan (1980, p. 74).
25 According to a Central Statistical Bureau report from 1978, the government allocated a budget of 104 million dirhams (equivalent in purchasing power to about £100 million today) to support media development (Ezzat, 1983, p. 36).
26 An exclusive, virtually all-male venue to which women's access is strictly limited.
27 Minister of Tolerance and Coexistence.
28 Minister of Foreign Affairs and International Cooperation.
29 Salama (2019).

30 UAE Ministry of Infrastructure Development (2007).
31 Moghadam (2003).
32 Ibid., p. 278.
33 Ibid., pp. 127, 130.
34 According to the National Bureau of Statistics, 737 Emirati women married foreigners in 2010, compared with 643 in 2009, an increase of almost 15 percent (Ismail, 2011).
35 Sputnik News Arabic (2017).
36 Cited in (Bailyn, 2016, p. 164).
37 Nazir and Tomppert (2011, p. 314).
38 Moghadam (2003, p. 115).
39 Ibid., p. 295).
40 Al Mazroui (2014).

References

Al Mazroui, A. (2014). 'The Gender Gap and the Women Who Fall Through It'. *The National*. 4 May. Available at: https://www.thenational.ae/the-gender-gap-and-the-women-who-fall-through-it-1.243851 [Accessed 13 July 2020].

Alrai. (2010). 'Lecture on Cultural Movement in the United Arab Emirates'. *Alrai*. Translated by the author. 13 October. Available at: http://alrai.com/article/422216/ [Accessed 27 August 2018].

Bailyn, L. (2016). *Breaking the Mold*. 2nd ed. Ithaca, NY: Cornell University Press.

Chehab, S. (2023). "Women Empowerment and Gender Balance: Soft Power Tools in UAE Foreign Policy." Anwar Gargash Diplomatic Academy. Available at: https://www.agda.ac.ae/docs/default-source/2023/women-empowerment-and-gender-balance--soft-power-tools-in-uae-foreign-policy.pdf?sfvrsn=c712673b_1

Ekerstedt, M. (2014). *Patriotism and Patriarchy: The Impact of Nationalism on Gender Equality*. Stockholm: The Kvinna Till Kvinna Foundation.

Ezzat, A. (1983). The Press in the Arab Gulf States: Part One [الصحافة في دول الخليج العربي الجزء الأول]. Translated by the author. Baghdad, Iraq: Gulf States Information Documentation Centre [مركز التوثيق الإعلامي لدول الخليج العربي].

Foley, S. (2010). *The Arab Gulf States: Beyond Oil and Islam*. Colorado, USA: Lynne Rienner Publishers Inc.

Forster, N. (2017). *A Quiet Revolution: The Rise of Women Managers, Business Owners and Leaders in The Arabian Gulf States*. Cambridge, UK: Cambridge University Press.

Ismail, M. (2011) 'More Emirati Women Marrying Foreigners'. *The National*. Available at: https://www.thenationalnews.com/uae/more-emirati-women-marrying-foreigners-1.443834#:~:text=According%20to%20the%20National%20Bureau,marry%20as%20they%20get%20older [Accessed: 21 June 2023].

Lerner, G. (1986). *The Creation of Patriarchy*. Oxford: Oxford University Press.

Moghadam, V. (2003). *Modernizing Women: Gender and Social Change in the Middle East*. Boulder, CO: L. Rienner.

Moheisen, E. (2015). 'Oil a Turning Point in the History of the UAE'. *Emarat Al Youm*. Translated by the author. 9 August. Available at: https://www.emaratalyoum.com/life/four-sides/2015-08-09-1.809802 [Accessed 27 August 2018].

Nafadi, A. (1996). *Journalism in the UAE: Origins, Technical and Historical Evolution*. Translated by the author. Abu Dhabi: UAE's Cultural Foundation Publications.

Nazir, S. and Tomppert, L. (2011). *Women's Rights in the Middle East and North Africa*. New York, NY: Freedom House.

Salama, S. (2019). 'President Decrees Changes into UAE Labor Laws to Boost Gender Equality'. *Gulf News*. 20 November. Available at: https://gulfnews.com/uae/government/president-decrees-changes-into-uae-labour-laws-to-boost-gender-equality-1.67956399 [Accessed 19 July 2020].

Salem, M. (2014). 'Hamama al Taniji Documenting Folk Medicine Tales in the UAE'. *Al Khaleej*. 16 October. Translated by the author. Available from http://www.alkhaleej.ae/supplements/page/d4b1325b-22f5-42f3-a398-1f14559f15ee [Accessed 22 August 2018].

Soffan, L. (1980). *Women of The United Arab Emirates*. London: Croom Helm Ltd.

Sonbol, A. (2012). *Gulf Women*. Doha, Qatar: Bloomsbury Qatar Foundation Publications.

Sputnik News Arabic (2017). 'Finally Resolving the Granting of Citizenship to Foreign Women in the UAE'. *Sputnik News Arabic*. 4 November. Translated by the author. Available at: https://arabic.sputniknews.com/arab_world/201711041027213151 [Accessed 31 August 2018].

Stephens, M. and Al Nahyan, S. (2018). 'Empowering Women in Remote Communities and Safeguarding Heritage'. *Mohammed Bin Rashid School of Government Publications*. April. Available at: https://www.mbrsg.ae/home/publications/case-studies/empowering-women-in-remote-communities-and-safegua.aspx [Accessed 10 May 2018].

UAE Ministry of Infrastructure Development (2007). UAE Labour Law. Available at: https://www.moid.gov.ae/Laws/UAE_Labour_Law.pdf [Accessed 23 July 2020].

World Economic Forum (2021). Global Gender Gap Report 2021. Available at: https://www.weforum.org/publications/global-gender-gap-report-2021 [Accessed 8 February 2024].

9 Conclusion

Women's experience of being subjected to oppression as othered inferiors is a universal challenge, influenced by the historical construct of patriarchy and the male hegemonic culture, in which their self-worth is diminished and their contributions are often unrecorded or marginalised. For a long time, patriarchal ideologies have hindered women's ability to assert their own identities and created gendered roles that women themselves have often accepted. Women's cooperation with the patriarchal system has strengthened its position. As Gerda Lerner has explained:

> This cooperation is secured by a variety of means: gender indoctrination, educational deprivation, the denial to women of knowledge of their history, the dividing of women, one from the other, by defining respectability and deviance according to women's sexual activities, by restraints and outright coercion, by discrimination in access to economic resources and political power, and by awarding class privileges to conforming women.[1]

The present study has shown, through participant observation and interviews with journalists, that Emirati women, like women elsewhere in the East and West, have been subjected to the ideologies of a patriarchal culture that have defined the media environment and newsroom practices, which are managed by executives closely aligned with an authoritarian regime.

These persistent ideologies have instituted stereotypical, gendered roles inside the Emirati newsrooms. As Stephanie M. Wildman describes, 'when women arrive in the workplace, the gendered expectation is that they will still perform that *caretaking* role'.[2] While the findings of this study reflect how versatile most Emirati and Arab expat journalists are, the female journalists interviewed clearly confirm that they are still challenged by a male hegemony that exposes them to sexism and limits their access to resources, meaningful reporting, and powerful positions in the newsroom.

Furthermore, the system of patriarchy, particularly the distinctive system of tribal patriarchalism in the Emirates, has fostered a patriotic journalistic practice that casts women as pillars of society in two restrictive ways. The first is biological, as they are—per Malin Ekerstedt—'responsible for the reproduction of the nation

DOI: 10.4324/9781003488415-9

by giving birth to new citizens'; the second is socio-cultural, as they are 'responsible for the continuation of national traditions, customs and morals'.[3] To support the Emirati leadership's strategy of developing a national identity, the practice of patriotic journalism, as this study has shown, has created a media environment that is devoid of criticism and overwhelmed by journalistic self-censorship. Any impulse towards the exercise of freedom of expression and the practice of serious investigative journalism in the Emirates is thwarted.

And now, more than ever, with the constant political changes in neighbouring countries like Saudi Arabia and Bahrain, the Emirates' involvement in the Yemen war and its humanitarian crisis, and the political boycott of Qatar, patriotism undermines authentic journalism, just as it did in America after the 9/11 terrorist attacks on the World Trade Center and Pentagon. Steered by the Emirati government, local media outlets and journalists have become involved in the creation of a framework of images, catchphrases, and content, often focused on the threat of terrorism, replete with expressions of integrity, honour, trust, and faith, in which God is associated with the nation or state.[4]

A pronouncement by an Emirati editor for the *Khaleej Times* exemplifies how patriotism influences journalism. Applying phrases like 'the evil media' and 'the malicious media' to outlets funded by regional and Western adversaries of the state, Mustafa Al Zarooni wrote that 'this media war between the good and evil came to maintain the national unity and the successful model the UAE is moulding, which is deemed a minaret in the region in terms of tolerance and respecting one another, and aimed to build a robust economy'.[5] In the current Emirati media environment, there is little chance for change, let alone for comprehensive transformation in press legislation and journalistic practice. Such calls as there are for transformation are met with the silent treatment from those who wield power, as Emirati commentator Mishaal Al Gergawi explains, 'to avoid feeding the issues at hand with more material that would in turn be debated and shared by local and foreign tweeters, bloggers, reporters, journalists and analysts. [They believe that] if an issue is ignored long enough, it will be rescinded from societal memory'.[6]

While the constitutional language applied to the mainstream media in the Emirates guarantees freedom of expression, it does not directly reference the press or journalism as a protected institution. In fact, Articles 30 and 31 of the Emirati constitution specifically state that 'freedom of opinion and expressing it verbally, in writing, or by other means of expression shall be guaranteed within the limits of law', and that 'freedom of communication by post, telegraph, or other means of communication, and the secrecy thereof, shall be guaranteed in accordance with law'.[7] Legal limitations on press practice have been enforced by many countries and were defined by the International Covenant on Civil and Political Rights of the Office of the United Nations High Commissioner for Human Rights in 1966. Belgium, for example, has enforced legal limitations on the press for societal protection under five specific categories: the rights of others, reputation management, national security, public order, and public health.[8]

In the Emirates, the combination of legal limitations on journalism practices on the basis of societal protection, social peace, and public decency, along with the strict de facto control imposed by the state over the press to sustain its authoritarian rule, has created a media environment that is engulfed by state-controlled propaganda and a newsroom culture in which journalists avoid investigative journalism and abandon their ethical role as watchdogs in fear of losing their jobs or even imprisonment and deportation. This particular aspect of the oppressive media environment, as well as the widespread ignorance of the remarkable role of Emirati journalists and intellectuals over the years, has been addressed by a number of Emirati journalists in social media recently. They collectively mourned the loss of pioneer Emirati journalists and authors such as Dr. Hussein Ghubash (1951–2020) and Thani Al Suwaidi (1966–2020) and blamed the patriarchal state, government-funded cultural authorities, and Emirati intellectuals for ignoring their historical contribution to journalism and literary and cultural movements in the UAE.

In a series of tweets, Emirati journalist and novelist Dhabiya Khamis chronicled her personal journey and cultural development in the UAE. She wrote:

> The first generation of literary modernity in the Emirates was a pioneer in its rebellion, its wording and its writing, criticizing and presenting new images of life and creativity, arguing with institutions, arguing with each other, and with itself. The first generation has a lot of internal freedom, but paid a high price for freedom by absentia, prevention, confiscation, and marginalization, unlike the current generation of tamed intellectuals. In fact, we, the Emirati literary writers of the eighties and nineties, were never treated with fairness. We were marginalized, while some suffered from bitter and incomprehensible hostilities that led to their isolation, displacement, writing anxiety and imprisonment. Our books were confiscated, banning the Emirati society from accessing our literary production. I was the first Emirati writer to be detained for publishing a journalistic feature under the title The Palm Graveyard in 1987. Unfortunately, our writers and ingenious intellectuals die without being recognized and their literary work unread by their people in the Emirates.[9]

Such stories are not unusual within the media landscape of the Arab Middle East, where the Arab public's consciousness is dominated by the fabrications of state-controlled print, broadcast, and social media platforms. This was a criticism made by Saudi journalist Jamal Khashoggi in his last column for *The Washington Post* before he was murdered in October 2018. Khashoggi wrote that:

> Arabs are either uninformed or misinformed. They are unable to adequately address, much less publicly discuss, matters that affect the region and their day-to-day lives. A state-run narrative dominates the public psyche, and while many do not believe it, a large majority of the population falls victim to this false narrative. Sadly, this situation is unlikely to change.[10]

Another problem that affects the quality of journalism in the Emirates and increases the authorities' control of the press is the outsourcing of news composition to communication and PR companies, who generate stories crafted to echo the authoritarian government's policies and agendas. Government officials, as well as local media corporations, deal closely with these PR companies to develop pre-fabricated messages and reports on matters both national and international that are meant to be the final word.

Emirati journalists themselves perceive the heavy presence of PR companies as usurping the role of journalism (see Chapter 5), which affects their work, threatens their careers, and impacts the quality of information as fake news increasingly predominates in the digital media age. In the Emirates, the mainstream media is now bursting with advertorials,[11] largely generated by PR firms, blurring the lines between journalism, marketing, and advertisement. Although they are funded by the government, local media outlets have succumbed to this burgeoning practice due to financial hardships, which have led them to seek additional income through direct marketing and advertising. Commenting on this challenge, which has resulted in the loss of a clear distinction between the mainstream media and PR companies in the Emirates, Ahmed Mustafa, a journalist for the Dubai-based *Gulf News*, wrote:

> Traditional media outlets started hiring PR and marketing professionals to help shape content in ways that can be monetized—especially on digital platforms. Media and PR: they need to refocus on their core businesses; PR as identity promoter and image builder, while media as a provider of credible news, information and analysis.[12]

The blurring of lines between the roles of PR companies and local mainstream media has led to an additional, serious ethical issue as journalists, PR professionals, and editors working for PR companies and media firms have become accustomed to receiving expensive corporate gifts from government and private entities in exchange for positive news coverage.

Even after the release of the Code of Ethics by the UAE Journalists' Association in 2007, which cautioned that 'accepting valuable cash and kind gifts may cause a journalist to be biased in his coverage and is considered a breach of the code', instances of bribery or the expectation of bribery have been reported by many journalists and PR professionals.[13] Mohammad Kirat, dean of the Communications Department at the University of Sharjah, revealed in a study that bribery amongst journalists and public relations professionals is quite common in the Emirates and the rest of the Arab Middle East. Kirat explained:

> Many journalists are quite noble, but in some newsrooms rampant bribery [both money and gifts] is a fiasco. The most egregious abuses occurred in the Arabic-language press. Some public relations practitioners complained that they have to play the game in order to get coverage of their product, company or event. They said that they feel powerless to change the situation.[14]

Memorably, a number of journalists disclosed experiences of bribery during their participation at Zayed University's Middle East Public Relations Association

Conference in 2012, where 'attendees reported that some public practitioners gave journalists iPhones, while others presented gift vouchers worth hundreds of dirhams'.[15] Some media observers, including journalists and PR professionals, have argued that this practice, which they prefer to call 'gifting', occurs due to the culture of giving and generosity in the Middle East and the Emirates in particular. Government and private entities might give journalists exclusive wares and electronic gadgets in exchange for positive press coverage at exhibitions, conferences, and corporate launches, or after the publication of a positive interview with a corporate executive or board member.

Outside the particular media landscape and newsroom culture of the Emirates, the legacy of traditional patriarchy persisted in the Middle East and tribal patriarchalism in the Arab Gulf states throughout the twentieth century and onward. This was exacerbated by the emergence of fundamentalist Salafism[16] as a political ideology in the early 1980s, which also saw the rise of extreme Islamist beliefs, including the doctrines of Iran's Grand Ayatollah Ruhollah Khomeini and the Islamist movement led by the Muslim Brotherhood. These political waves encouraged the formation of Muslim Sisterhood activism across the region and advanced reactionary ideologies, particularly with regard to women's affairs. These included strict sexual segregation, the division of public duties based on gender, and promotion of the idea that home is the best place for a woman and that her primary role is to be honourable and produce offspring.

As a result, gender has been politicised, and the lack of a collective response by Arab women to the ongoing socio-political changes in the Middle East and Arab Gulf states, despite their state-backed education and scholarships, has negatively affected their status. In particular, this has meant the policing—or amending—of their rights in family and labour laws. In Kuwait, for instance, seemingly minor issues like organising sport classes for school girls led to a parliamentary debate when the Islamist MP Issa Al Kandari proposed a law to limit women's participation in physical sports, including the Olympics, in respect of their 'nature' and in accordance with Kuwait's religious principles, traditions, and social values.[17]

Since the 1980s, Salafi fundamentalists (many of whom occupy significant positions as clerics or *mufti* in the Fatwa Department and have a prominent voice at royal courts), backed by patriarchal states such as the Emirates, have advocated an Islamic identity in which 'Muslims must return to a fixed tradition'.[18] In this tradition, the Muslim woman's honour must be protected in both the private sphere, through her demure behaviour as a daughter, mother, and wife, and the public, through her veiled appearance, which reflects her moral virtue and purity. And ever since, the leadership in the Emirates, like elsewhere in the oil-rich Gulf States, has promoted this vision as a political strategy to maintain and legitimate its political power.

In the Emirates, the threat of losing the nation's political autonomy and cultural identity has also led the leaders to Islamise feminism, but this has not changed the structure of tribal patriarchalism. On the one hand, Emirati women have become visibly integrated in the public sphere through access to education, employment, and political activity; on the other hand, they have become increasingly trapped in the confines of tribal-arranged marriages (central to tribal belonging via the maintenance of blood ties; see Chapter 7), some at a very young age, and trapped in roles determined for them by male relatives who abide by misinterpreted religious texts and traditional values, with no right to choose.

There is no simple, universal formula to follow for moving beyond tribal patriarchalism and implementing social change. Emirati society, despite its constant display of unity and cohesion, is a stratified society that appraises an individual's identity based on their tribal class. This evident stratification has resulted in the exclusion of middle-class Emirati men and women, in particular, from the process of national development, as they are often unseen and their voices unheard.

Yes, middle-class Emiratis are by and large financially secure in their employment; however, they feel inferior and socially unrecognised due to their low familial status as a result of their unknown or unimportant tribal affiliations. For middle-class Emiratis, social recognition is achieved solely through education and a successful career, in comparison with upper-class Emiratis, who are recognised for their prominent kinship, family wealth, alliances via marriage with other prominent tribes, and close ties with the monarchy, which grants them access to influential political positions. This is the basis of the class structure in the Emirates, as it is in the other Arab Gulf states. With the absence of poverty amongst the citizens of these oil-rich states, there is no visible lower class. Therefore, class is formed based on social status rather than income.

Steering civil social change is achievable if Emirati women of all social classes, but particularly those who belong to the demographically predominant group of middle-class tribes, act collectively. Currently, these Emirati women are functioning dynamically in the cultural and literary scenes, but there is no collective purpose or organisation in the picture. The marginal exception to this is the General Women's Union, which has been chaired by the former president's wife since 1975 and promotes women's heritage and traditional roles in society. Emirati women don't have a solid platform to convey their opinions on their rights, governance, and social justice in comparison with their peers elsewhere in the Middle East, including neighbouring Gulf states like Kuwait and Bahrain, who have succeeded in building feminist movements and stirring debates on social change over the past four decades.

Emirati women of all social classes need to collectively launch domestic feminist movements and NGOs to influence the national political landscape and increase their presence and participation in the regional and international arenas, building solidarity with their peers. Their contributions to literature and filmmaking, as well as the press, will bring further attention to their rights and eventually put pressure on the government to adopt new policies, which in due course will result in progressive civil and social changes. As Palestinian author Hisham Sharabi states, 'the women's movement is the detonator which will explode neo-patriarchal society from within. If allowed to grow and come into its own, it will become the permanent shield against patriarchal regression, the cornerstone of future modernity'.[19]

The United Arab Emirates is in a state of transitional progress. Bargaining with the patriarchy, at the core of a conservative tribal society that has only embraced modernity and adapted to the rapidly changing conditions of contemporary life in the past 50 years, will continue to be a challenge. But the commitment of the current leadership to educating the new generation of Emiratis and investing in a knowledge-based economy for the coming decades will surely continue to raise the status of Emirati women, who are being encouraged to forge ahead and assume prominent positions in non-traditional fields, including politics and diplomatic affairs.

The desire to appear modern is not only determined by the leadership but is also present in the private sphere, where concepts of patriarchy clash with the values of today's highly educated Emirati families, who champion Emirati women's education at home and abroad, support Emirati women's empowerment (which, of course, demonstrates loyalty to the leadership's wise policies), and defy outworn traditions such as tribal marriages and polygamy. To the older generation and those who adhere to the old school of thought, this acceptance of modernity amongst Emirati families can be tolerated insofar as the new values and associated practices do not 'contradic[t] Islamic law regarding family life'.[20]

Exploring the situation of Emirati women, especially those working in journalism, from multiple perspectives makes it clear that they must strive for collective consciousness to narrow their social and economic class divides. Women's solidarity is the key to undoing tribal patriarchalism and the deep-rooted cultural biases against women in the Emirates. Only when it is achieved—only when there are meaningful improvements to gender education and the legal rights of women within the family law—will social transformation be possible within Emirati society and the progression from patriarchy to gender equality be realised.

Notes

1 Lerner (1986, p. 217).
2 Lerner (1986, p. 200).
3 Ekerstedt (2014, p. 4).
4 Cherkaoui (2017, p. 4).
5 Zarooni (2018).
6 Al Gergawi (2011).
7 Duffy (2014, pp. 27, 28).
8 Duffy (2014).
9 Khamis (2020). The series of tweets was posted on 6 July and 21 July 2020. Translated by the author.
10 Khashoggi (2018).
11 Advertorials are advertisements produced in the format of journalistic content.
12 Mustafa (2018).
13 Duffy (2014, p. 26).
14 Duffy (2012).
15 Ibid.
16 A hybrid of Wahabism and conservative Islam, Salafism is a revivalist movement formed by Sunni theologians between the 1970s and 1980s. It remains widely popular in the Arab Gulf states.

17 Al Suwailan (2006).
18 Ibid., p. 138.
19 Sharabi (1988, p. 154).
20 Soffan (1980, p. 102).

References

Al Gergawi, M. (2011). 'Incommunicado: The State of the Gulf'. *Gulf News*. 17 April. Available at: https://gulfnews.com/opinion/op-eds/incommunicado-the-state-of-the-gulf-1.794063 [Accessed 6 May 2019].

Al Suwailan, Z. (2006). *The Impact of Societal Values on Kuwaiti Women and the Role of Education*. Knoxville, TN: Department of Philosophy, University of Tennessee. Tennessee Research and Creative Exchange (TRACE). August. Available at: http://trace.tennessee.edu/cgi/viewcontent.cgi?article=3141&context=utk_graddiss [Accessed 8 April 2019].

Cherkaoui, T. (2017). *The News Media at War: The Clash of Western and Arab Networks in the Middle East*. New York, NY: I.B. Tauris.

Duffy, M. (2012). 'Journalists Should Never Compromise on Integrity'. *Gulf News*. 9 March. Available at: https://gulfnews.com/opinion/op-eds/journalists-should-never-compromise-on-integrity-1.991869 [Accessed 8 May 2019].

Duffy, M. (2014). *Media Law in the United Arab Emirates*. Alphen aan den Rijn, the Netherlands: Kluwer Law International.

Ekerstedt, M. (2014). *Patriotism and Patriarchy: The Impact of Nationalism on Gender Equality*. Stockholm: Kvinna Till Kvinna Foundation.

Khamis, D. (2020). X (formerly Twitter) account. Available at http://www.twitter.com/dhabiya1 [Accessed 6 July 2020].

Khashoggi, J. (2018). 'Jamal Khashoggi's Final Column: "What the Arab World Needs Most Is Free Expression"'. *The Independent*. 18 October. Available at: https://www.independent.co.uk/news/world/americas/jamal-khashoggi-final-washington-post-column-death-missing-saudi-arabia-journalist-a8589456.html [Accessed 12 February 2019].

Lerner, G. (1986). *The Creation of Patriarchy*. Oxford: Oxford University Press.

Mustafa, A. (2018). 'Blurring Lines between Journalism, Marketing and Advertisement'. *Gulf News*. 10 December. Available at: https://gulfnews.com/opinion/op-eds/blurring-lines-between-journalism-marketing-and-advertisement-1.60835681 [Accessed 7 May 2019].

Sharabi, H. (1988). *Neopatriarchy: A Theory of Distorted Change in Arab Society*. Oxford: Oxford University Press.

Soffan, L. (1980). *Women of the United Arab Emirates*. London: Croom Helm Ltd.

Zarooni, M. (2018). 'UAE Media Stands Guard against Fake News'. *Khaleej Times*. 15 April. Available at: https://www.khaleejtimes.com/kt-40-anniversary/20180415/uae-media-stands-guard-against-fake-news [Accessed 8 May 2019].

Appendix
Study Details

Participant observation

Locations:

1 Dubai News Centre, operated by Dubai Media Incorporated
2 Abu Dhabi News Centre, operated by Abu Dhabi Media Company

Duration:

Four months, from October 2016 through January 2017, for 14 days at each news centre, excluding the weekend (Fridays and Saturdays). To conduct the observation, I spent two hours monitoring the afternoon shift and the live news broadcast at 8:00 pm local time.

Semi-structured interviews

The semi-structured interviews were recorded with a voice recorder and a voice recording app on my smartphone, as a backup, after obtaining the interviewees' consent. The interviews were conducted between 15 February and 1 May 2017 in private meeting rooms at the respective interviewees' workplaces.

Gender:

- 30 females
- 10 males

Stratification:

- Early generation (1970s–1990s), between the ages of 30 and 60
- New generation (2000s–onward), in their 20s

Nationalities represented:

1 Emirati
2 Jordanian

3   Moroccan
4   Syrian
5   Egyptian
6   Iraqi
7   Palestinian

Media corporations represented:

1   Abu Dhabi Television Channel One
2   Emirates News Agency (WAM)
3   *Al Ittihad* daily newspaper (Abu Dhabi)
4   *Al Bayan* daily newspaper (Dubai)
5   *Al Khaleej* daily newspaper (Sharjah)
6   *Al Roeya* daily newspaper (Abu Dhabi)
7   *Zahrat Al Khaleej* women's weekly magazine (Abu Dhabi)
8   *Al Azminah Al Arabiya* weekly magazine (Sharjah)
9   *Awraq* weekly magazine (Sharjah)

List of journalists interviewed

Note: in the age column, a dash indicates that the journalist did not wish to reveal their age.
Females:

Name	Age	Job Title	Nationality
Fatema Al Senani	34	Head of Operations Projects	Emirati
F.H. (Pseudonym)	34	TV Presenter	Emirati
J.M. (Pseudonym)	55	Reporter	Emirati
Huda Al Kubaisi	—	Reporter	Emirati
Hana Al Hamadi	45	Senior Journalist	Emirati
Mona Al Hmoudi	27	Journalist Investigation	Emirati
Badria Al Kassar	—	Journalist	Emirati
Ameena Awadh Bin Amro	38	Head of Electronic Publishing	Emirati
Mahra Al Jenaibi	28	Reporter	Emirati
Rawdha (Pseudonym)	35	Journalist	Emirati
Heyam Obaid Bawazir	41	Head of News Output	Emirati
Hala Al Gergawi	35	Executive Managing Editor & Editor-in-Chief	Emirati
Yaqoutah Abdulla Al Dhanhane	28	Journalist	Emirati
Leila (Pseudonym)	36	Executive News Editor	Emirati
Yusra Adil	29	Senior News Anchor & Editor, External Politics	Emirati
Moza Fikri	54	Digital Media Managing Editor	Emirati
Bashayer (Pseudonym)	27	Translation Managing Editor	Emirati
Shamsa Saif Al Hanaee	29	Sports Reporter	Emirati
Reem Al Breiki	41	Senior Business Journalist	Emirati
Fedaa Mershid	47	News Monitor	Emirati

(Continued)

Name	Age	Job Title	Nationality
Mahra (Pseudonym)	65	Former Senior Journalist & Editor-in-Chief	Emirati
Rasha Tubeileh	34	Journalist	Jordanian
Hala Al Khayyat	39	Journalist	Jordanian
Jalila (Pseudonym)	—	Editor	Jordanian
Najat Fares Al Fares	48	Journalist	Jordanian
K.T. (Pseudonym)	47	Senior Journalist	Moroccan
Laila Hafez	—	Journalist	Egyptian
Lahib Abdulkhaliq	60	Editor, External Politics	Iraqi
Muna Saeed Al Taher	62	Field Reporter	Iraqi
Alaa Abed Al Ghani	29	Journalist	Syrian

Males:

Name	Age	Job Title	Nationality
Mohamed Al Hammadi	—	Editor-in-Chief	Emirati
Abdulla Abdulkarim	38	Senior Editor, Economy News	Emirati
Ali Al Amoudi	60	Senior Journalist	Emirati
Dr. Hussain Abdulqader Harhara	58	Finance Managing Editor	Emirati
Salam Abu Shihab	52	Manager of Abu Dhabi Bureau	Palestinian
A.D. (Pseudonym)	38	Business Reporter	Palestinian
Yousef Bustangi	56	Business Reporter	Palestinian
Abady Mohamed Ali	60	Senior Sports Journalist	Egyptian
Reda El Bawardy	36	Senior Field Reporter	Egyptian
Alsayed Salama	51	Senior Journalist	Egyptian

Interview questions

1 When did you start your career? And could you walk us through your academic background, please.
2 What are the most memorable achievements of your career?
3 Could you describe the challenges of being a journalist in the Emirates? What about the presence of PR agencies, do you find it challenging?
4 Were there any life-changing experiences in this profession that you can share with us?
5 What are the types of topics that you often discussed in the stories or features that you wrote?
6 Did you face some level of resistance in terms of content? Or were some of the stories or features that you drafted banned from publication at some point? If so, why?
7 What are a few of the hardships you've faced from being in the public eye as a journalist, and how did you overcome them?
8 (For female journalists only:) Did you find it challenging being taken seriously by your male colleagues in terms of the hard-hitting, socio-economic, and political stories you wanted to cover? Were your professionalism and work judged

negatively, or have you gone through physical harassment for working as a journalist?

9   Do you think that journalism as a profession is gendered?

10 Career-wise, do you think that you are compensated enough for your work?

11 How would you describe journalism as a profession and a practice in the Emirates (e.g., freedom of speech, writing, and expression)?

12 Do you feel threatened by the media law (the 1980 Press and Publication Law) or the media authorities (censorship in particular)? If so, would you mind telling us a story of an experience that you've been through with the media authorities in the Emirates?

13 With the increasing debate on social media replacing journalism, do you think that it has affected the way journalists receive, gather, and distribute news? What does it mean for the future of news?

14 How do social media and other web technologies (e.g., blogs) affect newsroom operations in reporting news events? Did it change the nature of breaking news and the natural role of 'the journalist'? (i.e., reporting, editing, etc.)

15 What advice can you offer Emirati journalists who are looking to do the same within their own professions?

16 Can you tell us about the advice you've picked up on landing your dream job as a journalist?

17 Can you describe your most important mentor and how they helped you achieve success as a journalist?

Index

Note: Page references with "n" denote endnotes.

For Product Safety Concerns and Information please contact our EU
representative GPSR@taylorandfrancis.com
Taylor & Francis Verlag GmbH, Kaufingerstraße 24, 80331 München, Germany

www.ingramcontent.com/pod-product-compliance
Ingram Content Group UK Ltd.
Pitfield, Milton Keynes, MK11 3LW, UK
UKHW021826240425
457818UK00006B/88

9 78 1 0 3 2 7 8 5 4 1 7